3

Using AACR2

Using AACR2

*A Step-by-Step Algorithmic Approach
to Part II of the Anglo-American Cataloguing Rules*

Malcolm Shaw
Bill Dent
David Evans
David Smith

THE LIBRARY
ASSOCIATION

First published 1980

British Library Cataloguing in Publication Data

Using AACR 2
    1. Anglo-American cataloguing rules, 1978
    2. Descriptive cataloguing
    I. Shaw, Malcolm   II. Library Association
    025.3'2   Z694

ISBN 0 85365 612 6 (Casebound)
     0 85365 622 3 (Paperback)

Designed by Ron Jones

Contents

Preface

This work had its origins in a discussion between David Smith, a lecturer in the School of Librarianship of Leeds Polytechnic, and Malcolm Shaw of the Polytechnic's Educational Technology Unit. The theme of the discussion was the need to evolve a teaching method for introducing students to what was (for the uninitiated at least) the bewildering ramifications of rules in the 1st edition of the Anglo-American Cataloguing Rules. Malcolm Shaw suggested the possibility of an algorithmic approach. i.e. a decision-making flow chart which would enable the Rules to be applied in a sequence of logical steps.

An algorithm to chapter 1 of the Rules was drafted, and used for a time in the School of Librarianship. Further development was deferred, however, because of the imminence of a 2nd edition of AACR. Subsequently David Evans and Bill Dent, also of the Leeds School of Librarianship, became interested in the project and the present collaboration resulted, once the text of the 2nd edition became available. The general division of work was that Malcolm Shaw drafted the outline of the algorithms for all the chapters covered by this introductory text — chapters 21-5. David Smith collaborated with him in producing the detailed version for chapter 21, and Bill Dent fulfilled a similar role in the cases of chapters 22-5. David Evans collected the accompanying examples and prepared the commentaries which relate to them. Bill Dent wrote the various introductory sections. However, at every stage there were discussions and mutually agreed amendments to the contents. The results amply fulfil AACR's definition of 'shared responsibility': unquestionably a situation in which Rule 21.6C2 may be deemed to apply!

The work consists of four parts:

(1) A brief introduction to 'author catalogues' and 'author cataloguing', intended mainly for people who are new to the subject. This section may be by-passed by more experienced cataloguers and by students who have received a general introduction to the matter.
(2) The algorithm. In fact, two algorithms: the first relating to
    chapter 21 — *Choice of access points*, and the second to
    chapters 22-5 — *Form of headings*.
(3) A collection of examples, presented in the form of facsimiles of title pages of books, etc., plus any additional information which will be necessary in cataloguing an item. The emphasis in the examples is upon monographs,

simply because the necessary data for these could be presented most conveniently and because, in any event, the decisions to be taken are independent of any particular kind of library material. The examples progress from the straightforward to the more complex: consequently they should be worked through in the order in which they appear. An additional reason for so doing is that some decisions in the later examples will be facilitated by having completed earlier ones. Having worked through one or both of the algorithms using a particular example you should check your decisions against the compilers' 'solutions' and commentary which will be found on p.165 et seq.

(4) 'Complete structures': these appear on p.128 and are summaries of Algorithms 1 and 2. They may be used for quick access to particular sections of the algorithms when you are thoroughly familiar with their overall organization and logic, or to re-locate your 'place' if you have lost your point of reference in the text. However, using the 'complete structures' too soon is likely to cause you to make incorrect assumptions and decisions due to ignorance of the basic principles contained in the algorithms.

The work is intended primarily for students of librarianship who are in process of initiation into the techniques of cataloguing. However, it is hoped that it will also be of value to practising cataloguers who are 'converting' from the use of AACR1, or some other code of practice, to AACR2. It is specifically a guide to the application of chapters 21-5 of the 2nd edition of the Anglo-American Cataloguing Rules, but there is an underlying intention to show that 'author cataloguing' involves a sequence of logical steps in arriving at the appropriate entries and headings for a document. At the same time it must be stressed that the work does relate directly to AACR2 as it stands. It has not been the intention to produce a general manual of cataloguing practice, nor was it considered appropriate to attempt to 'improve' upon the Rules.

Acknowledgements are due to the following publishers, who gave permission for the reproduction of the title pages from their publications: Oxford University Press; Macmillan & Co.Ltd.; Basil Blackwell and Mott, Ltd.; Earth Island, Ltd.; W.H. Allen & Co.Ltd.; University of California Press; E.F.N. Spon, Ltd.; Vacation-Work; Cambridge University Press; Frederick Warne & Co.Ltd.; Penguin Books, Ltd.; The New American Library of World Literature, Inc.; Uitgeverij Het Spectrum; William Collins, Sons & Co.Ltd.; The Catholic Truth Society; New English Library, Ltd.; Marshall Morgan & Scott, Ltd.; Hutchinson & Co.Ltd.; Sweet & Maxwell, Ltd.; Her Majesty's Stationery Office; Tropical Products Institute; Blandford Press Ltd.; Dover Publications, Inc.; The Decca Record Co.Ltd. In addition we wish to thank the British, Canadian and American Library Associations for their permission to quote extensively from AACR2 itself.

Author catalogues
and author cataloguing

A library catalogue consists of a file of *entries* or *records* of materials contained in a library. Each entry contains a certain amount of information about the item recorded: sufficient to —

(a) Identify the document. i.e. To distinguish it from any other item and, further, to distinguish one edition or version of a work from other editions or versions of the same work, and

(b) Characterize the document. i.e. Convey some impression of the nature of the work — both its physical make-up and its intellectual content.

Note that the term 'document' is used to imply an item of library material in any form: a book, a piece of music, a map, a sound recording, etc, etc.

The information which is contained in a catalogue entry is called the *description*. It comprises all the information contained in the entry other than the *heading*: the data element by which the entry is arranged in the catalogue file. The process of preparing the description is referred to, naturally enough, as *descriptive cataloguing*. A typical catalogue entry might appear thus:

The
description

> ?? Heading ??
>
> Four hundred years of English education [text] / by W.H.G. Armytage. — 2nd ed. — Cambridge : Cambridge U.P., 1970.
> xii, 353 p. ; 22 cm.
> First published 1964.
> ISBN 0-521-09583-2

The amount of descriptive detail which is necessary in a catalogue entry will vary according to the size and purpose of the library. Further, the order and fashion in which the description is presented is not, in itself, of any great significance. However, it may be apparent that it is desirable for such data to be given in a standard and consistent manner, not merely within one particular catalogue but in all catalogues and similar bibliographic listings. Consequently there are codes of rules which prescribe the way in which cataloguers should express the descriptive data. In the 2nd edition of the Anglo-American Cataloguing Rules (subsequently referred to as AACR2), with which this text is concerned, Part I sets out the rules for the descriptive cataloguing of all types of library materials. However, the present work is concerned with the *choice* and *form* of headings in 'author' and 'title' catalogues.

The headings which are assigned to the catalogue entries described above will depend upon the objectives of the catalogues involved. Broadly, the basic objectives of library catalogues are:

(a) To enable the location of library materials on a particular subject or subject area. e.g. Materials on underground railways, electric railways, railway locomotives, or on railways in general, or, for that matter, on the subject of transportation in general. The kind of catalogue which provides for this sort of approach is, obviously enough, a *subject catalogue*, in which the headings will be labels which identify, in one way or another, the subject matter of the document recorded. The subject catalogue and its construction is outside the scope of the present text.

(b) To permit the location of a particular document, about which some precise identifying feature is known. e.g. The name of the person or persons, organization or organizations, in some way responsible for the creation of the document; its title; or the title of the series of documents to which it belongs. An alternative way of describing this objective would be to say that the library catalogue should provide for a *known-item search*. The kind of catalogue which caters for this sort of approach is generally referred to as an 'author' or 'author/title' catalogue. The headings in such a catalogue will, then, be names of people or organizations responsible for the content of documents and the titles of both individual items and series of items. It is with the establishment of such headings that the present text is concerned: more particularly, with Part II of AACR2, which governs the choice of these headings and the form which they take.

Before proceeding further it will be useful to define more precisely the terms 'author' and 'author catalogue'.

Authorship

'Personal author' is defined by Rule 21.1A1 of AACR2 in the following way:
    A personal author is the person chiefly responsible for the creation of the intellectual content of a work. For example, writers of books and composers of music are the authors of the works they create; compilers of bibliographies are the authors of those bibliographies; cartographers are the authors of their maps; artists and photographers of the works they create. In addition, in certain cases, performers are the authors of sound recordings, films, and videorecordings.
    Further, in Rule 21.1B2, AACR2 recognizes that in certain instances corporate bodies (or organizations) may be regarded as being, effectively,

'authors' of certain categories of document which emanate from them. Thus 'author', in the sense in which it is used in the Rules and in this text, has a much wider connotation than merely 'writer of the text of a book'.

'Author catalogue'

It follows, from what has been said above, that a so-called 'author catalogue' is rather more than its name suggests. It will contain entries under the names of people (and organizations) who are in some way responsible for the existence of a document, and via whom a catalogue user may reasonably consult the catalogue in making a 'known-item' search.

In addition, as indicated earlier, the 'author catalogue' may well include entries under the titles of works and under the titles of series to which those works belong. These 'title' entries may be arranged in a separate sequence to form an independent 'title catalogue', but are more often filed in the same sequence as the 'author' entries to produce a single alphabetical sequence of 'author' and 'title' entries. This is usually referred to as simply an 'author catalogue', but it would be more exactly described as an 'author/title catalogue'.

It should be remembered that most 'author catalogues' are multiple entry catalogues. That is to say, they will usually contain a number of entries for the same item under different headings. e.g. a book written by two authors, with significant illustrative content by a third person, and belonging to a bibliographic series such as 'The new naturalist series', might well have five entries in the 'author catalogue': under the names of its two authors, under the name of the illustrator, under its title, and under the title of the series. Generally one of these entries will be regarded as the *main entry* for the document: the principal entry; that which will contain the fullest information in a catalogue which (perhaps to economize in the use of space) does not give full descriptive details in all entries. The cataloguer will attempt to ensure that the heading of the main entry is the principal identifying feature for the work. The additional entries made for an item (i.e. those other than the main entry) are referred to as *added entries*. They may contain rather less descriptive information than the main entry for the document.

The convention of having an 'author catalogue' made up of main and added entries is long established. It probably dates from the 19th century when catalogues were frequently in book format, produced by conventional printing methods, and it was desirable to restrict the physical size of catalogues as much as possible. Whatever the origin of the convention, the need to distinguish a main entry from the other entries made for a work is questioned with increasing frequency. Certainly the selection of the main entry heading from a number of headings which may be considered to be necessary for a work is often the most difficult part of the author cataloguing process. Paragraph 0.5 of the general introduction to AACR2 makes a brief mention of the principle of main entry, and fuller discussions may be found in the other readings cited at the end of this introductory section. It is not felt that this is an appropriate place to debate the question. However, it should be noted that whilst distinguishing between main and added entries may make little difference to the effectiveness of an individual library catalogue, the assignment of a main entry *heading* is an attempt to establish a standard identifying label by which a work will be listed in *all* bibliographic listings — library catalogues, bibliographies, publishers' lists, etc. — not all of which are multiple entry listings.

In addition to main and added entries an 'author catalogue' will contain *references*. These may be *see* or *see also* references. The purposes of the two kinds of references are quite distinct. A *see* reference is a firm direction away from a heading which is not used and will never be used to a preferred heading. e.g.

> Clemens, Samuel Langhorne
> *see*
> Twain, Mark.

This implies that the author's real name — Samuel Langhorne Clemens — will never be used as a heading for entries: his pseudonym — Mark Twain — will always be used in its stead.

A *see also* reference is employed to link two headings which are (or may be) both used as headings for entries, and between which some connection exists. e.g.

> Great Britain. *Countryside Commission*
> *see also*
> Great Britain. *National Parks Commission*
> for publications before 1967.

It should be stressed that references are used only for the two purposes outlined above. They are not used to provide access points to a document from alternative identifying features. e.g. A work entitled 'The Penguin book of Elizabethan verse', compiled by Edward Lucie-Smith would (according to AACR2) have its main entry under its title. An added entry would certainly be made under the heading for the name of the compiler — Lucie-Smith, Edward. A *see* reference would be made to direct the catalogue user away from the unused form of Lucie-Smith's name to the preferred form. i.e.

> Smith, Edward Lucie-
> *see*
> Lucie-Smith, Edward.

A reference should *not* be used, however, to provide access via Lucie-Smith's name. i.e.

> Lucie-Smith, Edward
> *see*
> The Penguin book of Elizabethan verse.

This would imply that the heading — Lucie-Smith, Edward — will never be used as a heading in its own right and that the name will only ever be associated in the catalogue with this one publication. This is clearly absurd since the individual concerned may have in the past, or may in the future, be responsible for other works recorded in the catalogue.

The need for a code of cataloguing rules

An 'author catalogue' is, then, a record of the materials held in a library, with entries under a variety of 'author' and title headings via which a cataloguer user may reasonably search for a work.

Whilst an 'author catalogue' is clearly an important element in the effective functioning of a library, its construction would seem to be a fairly straight-forward process of listing or inventorying. Therefore the need for an extensive code of practice such as the Anglo-American Cataloguing Rules may come as something of a surprise to the newcomer to cataloguing. It would seem possible to base the construction of such a catalogue upon a single, simple, direction to the effect of:

> Enter a work under the name of its author (the person responsible for its creation): in the absence of any attribution of authorship, enter the work under its title.

For a not insignificant proportion of the material which most libraries catalogue this simple direction may, indeed, suffice. However, it is equally probable that in compiling even a very short list of 10 or 20 books and/or other library materials there will arise situations in which we must make decisions beyond the terms of this simple direction. Naturally, the need for these extra decisions increases when our listing consists of thousands, or tens of thousands, of items – as in a large library catalogue.

The instances in which these further decisions must be taken may be analyzed as follows:

(a) When the cataloguer is *uncertain whom to regard as 'author'.* e.g. when a number of people share the responsibility for the contents of a work. Instances of this are when two or more individuals jointly prepare a work; or where a work is a collection of contributions from a number of different people. Another example of where this problem arises is in the case of what AACR2 refers to as 'mixed authorship'. That is to say, where two or more people have contributed to the contents of a work in different ways. Instances of this would be a work in which one person contributed the words and another composed the music; or in which one person provided the illustrations and another the accompanying text.

It is worth noting that the question really at issue here is that concerning the main entry heading. If one assumes a multiple entry catalogue, one presumes that entries will be made under any of the names or other identifying features via which a document may be sought. Therefore, in asking 'Whom do I regard as author?' one is really asking 'Whom (or what) do I select as main entry heading, and, under whom (or what) shall I make added entries?'.

(b) When there is *uncertainty concerning the name to be used as the heading for an author.* Specifically, these uncertainties may arise because:

    (i) An author has used different names,, e.g. family name *and* title of nobility — Anthony Eden *and* Lord Avon; real name *and* pseudonym — Charles Dodgson *and* Lewis Carroll; maiden *and* married name(s) — Jacqueline Bouvier, Jacqueline Kennedy, Jacqueline Onassis; and so on.

    (ii) Different forms of the same name may occur, e.g. variations in fullness — A. Conan Doyle *and* Sir Arthur Conan Doyle; the name in different languages — Jeanne d'Arc *and* Joan of Arc; different transliterations of the same name — Mohammed, Mahommed, Mahomet; and so on.

    (iii) The entry element for the name is not obvious., e.g. compound names — Cecil Woodham-Smith: entered as Woodham-Smith, Cecil, or as Smith, Cecil Woodham- ? ; names with prefixes — Charles de Gaulle: entered as de Gaulle, Charles, or as Gaulle, Charles de? , a given name or bye-name — William of Malmesbury: entered under Malmesbury, William of, or in direct order?

      Generally names from different cultures may pose problems to the cataloguer , e.g. a Chinese name such as Foo Kwac Wah: which part of the name is to be regarded as 'surname' and the entry element for the name?

      It should be borne in mind that uncertainties about names apply equally — or perhaps to an even greater extent — to corporate names: names of organizations and other bodies. e.g. the British Department of Education and Science: should it be entered as — Department of Education and Science, or as Education and Science, Department of, or under some other form of name?

      Similarly, the Association of Assistant Librarians is a sub-section of the (British) Library Association. Should this organization be entered directly under its own name or as a sub-heading of the parent organization — Library Association. *Association of Assistant Librarians?*

(c) Finally, when an entry is required under title (either as a main or added entry heading) the cataloguer may need to establish *which title* to use, in that the titles of works may alter in the same way as the names of authors. Consider the hundreds of different titles which have appeared on different versions and editions of the Bible and its constituent parts over the centuries, or the many different titles which have been applied to editions of anonymous classics such as *The Arabian nights.*

The problems outlined and illustrated above are, in themselves, very minor matters. However, it is perhaps apparent that in a library catalogue containing many thousands of entries, built over a long period of time, by many different hands, unless these problems – small though they may be – are solved in a consistent fashion then the catalogue as a whole will be inconsistent and contradictory and unpredictable and, as a consequence, inefficient and unreliable.

The purpose of a code of rules for 'author' cataloguing is, then, to establish a consistent and standard practice in the *choice* of headings and in establishing the *form* which those headings will take. The primary objective is the obvious one of achieving consistency and uniformity within a particular catalogue. However, there is an underlying objective of much broader significance: the establishment of a standard practice in library catalogues and other bibliographic listings on a national and, hopefully, an international scale. In short, to ensure that a document will be entered in precisely the same fashion in any catalogue or listing in which it appears. Clearly it would be convenient for a number of reasons if this were so. For example it would simplify the checking of bibliographic data and it would facilitate the interchange of cataloguing data between libraries and cataloguing agencies.

Evolution of AACR2

It would seem that libraries have employed cataloguing rules – albeit perhaps very simple 'house rules' of purely local significance – for hundreds of years. Presumably from the time that the size of collections necessitated some measure of sophistication in the way in which they were recorded.

However, it was not until the second half of the 19th century that codes of rules with greater than local influence began to emerge. The starting point, what may be regarded as the foundation of modern 'author cataloguing' practice, was the publication in 1841 of 'Rules for the compilation of the printed catalogues of the British Museum'. Subsequently various other collections of rules of national or international significance appeared. C.A. Cutter's 'Rules for a dictionary catalog', published in the United States in 1876, and the German language 'Prussian Instructions' (1899), widely influential in Central Europe and German-speaking countries, are examples. Both the American and the British Library Associations (in 1879 and 1883 respectively) produced their own codes of rules.

In the early years of the 20th century the two last named Associations were individually contemplating revision of their respective sets of rules. The possibility of a joint code, representing, effectively, a standard code of cataloguing practice for the English-speaking world was proposed. The result was *Cataloguing rules: author and title entries,* published in 1908, and more frequently referred to as the 'A.A. (Anglo-American) Code', the '1908 Code', or the 'Joint Code'. This remained the basis for 'author' and descriptive cataloguing, in Britain at least, for almost 60 years.

Some tentative moves towards a joint revision of the '1908 Code' were made in the 1930s, but World War II intervened. The American Library Association went ahead alone with the revision: the outcome being the *A.L.A.*

Cataloguing Rules published in 1949. This revision made little impact in Britain, but was critically received in the United States; chiefly because it represented a considerable increase in size and complexity over the '1908 Code'. One of the foremost critics was Seymour Lubetzky, whose views were trenchantly expressed in *Cataloguing rules and principles: a critique of the A.L.A. rules for entry and a proposed design for their revision*, published in 1953. The 'proposed design for their revision' was based upon the identification of broad, basic cataloguing problems (or bibliographic conditions, as Lubetzky called them) instead of upon an attempt to enumerate specific problems and situations (or cases), which had been the approach of all earlier codes of cataloguing rules.

The American Library Association then embarked upon a further revision of their rules, with Lubetzky's ideas as a basis. During this process the committees of the British and Canadian Library Associations which were concerned with rules revision began to co-operate with their counterparts in the United States. Eventually, in 1967, the 'new' code appeared: now officially entitled *Anglo-American Cataloguing Rules.* Unfortunately, whilst there was a very considerable measure of trans-Atlantic agreement, the 'Rules' appeared in two versions: a British and a North American text. An influential factor had been a Statement of Principles which had emerged from an international conference on cataloguing principles held in Paris in 1961. This set out various principles concerning catalogue. construction, aimed at establishing international uniformity of practice in the making of catalogues and bibliographies.

Even before this 1st edition of AACR appeared the British and American Library Associations had made an agreement to jointly monitor the application of the new rules and to discuss (without necessarily agreeing upon) any possible amendments. Between 1969 and 1974 a number of changes were agreed and promulgated in amendment bulletins. The most significant change was the complete revision of chapter 6 — the rules for the descriptive cataloguing of monographs — in order to establish conformity with the International Standard Bibliographic Description (Monographs). The latter was the first in a series of standards, prepared under the auspices of the International Federation of Library Associations and Institutions (IFLA), intended, as the name implies, to further international uniformity in the structure of records for library materials. The revision of chapter 6 was published in 1974 as a replacement fascicule for the original chapter.

Then, in 1974, a tripartite agreement was made between representatives of Canada, the United Kingdom and the United States to embark upon a 2nd edition of AACR. The delegates at the meeting represented both the library associations and the national libraries of the three countries. A Joint Steering Committee for Revision of AACR (JSCAACR) was set up to co-ordinate the work, and also various national revision committees were appointed in the three countries involved.

The decision to revise the code of practice, such a relatively short time after the publication of the 1st edition, was viewed with a certain amount of disquiet by some librarians. However, arguably unfortunately, the implications of revision do not seem to have been very fully considered in libraries until the work of revision was completed and the 2nd edition published. Only since then has there been some concerted questioning as to whether this is an appropriate time to revise cataloguing practice, however theoretically desirable some of the changes might be. The decisions of the British Library, the Library of Congress, and the National Library of Canada to implement AACR2 for their centrally produced bibliographic records with effect from January 1981 obviously has considerable significance for the increasing number of libraries which are heavily dependent upon central agencies for their cataloguing services.

It is not the intention to discuss the arguments for and against the adoption of AACR2 in this present context. Whatever the practical difficulties which it poses, the objectives underlying the new edition are, in principle, very justifiable. They are to:

(a) Reconcile the British and North American texts of AACR: not only in decisions but also in presentation and expression.
(b) Consolidate the amendments made since 1969.
(c) Incorporate the international standards which had emerged since 1967. In the main this relates to the various International Standard Bibliographic Descriptions referred to earlier. Specifically: a generalized specification for the description of bibliographic and library materials — ISBD(G); for monographs — ISBD(M); for non-book materials — ISBD(NBM); for cartographic materials — ISBD(CM); and for serials — ISBD(S). Two further standards — for music and for 'old books' are in preparation.
(d) Introduce fuller and more integrated provision for non-book materials: the importance of which, in libraries, had increased rapidly since 1967.
(e) Provide for the machine processing of cataloguing data, which was just beginning to develop during the period when AACR1 was in preparation.

AACR2 was published at the end of 1978, after a considerably shorter gestation period than any of its direct predecessors. However, it should be recognized that AACR2 is *not* a new code: it is a revision of an existing corpus of rules.

Structure of AACR2

The basic structure of AACR2 is different from that of AACR1. In AACR1 the outline structure is:

Part I	Rules for entry and heading: the *choice* and *form of headings.*
Part II	Rules for the descriptive cataloguing of books and book-like materials.
Part III	Rules for the (mainly descriptive) cataloguing of non-book materials.

In AACR2 the outline structure is:

Part I	Rules for description. These are set out in a general chapter which applies to all types of library material, supplemented by a series of chapters dealing with the description of particular forms of library materials.
Part II	Rules for the establishment of headings: a single collection of rules which apply to all kinds of materials.

The details of the organization and application of Part I – the rules for description – are not the concern of the present text, and will not be considered in any further detail.

The outline of Part II is as follows:

Chapter 20	Introduction to Part II.
Chapter 21	Access points (i.e. decisions on *what* entries should be made for a document.)
Chapters 22-5	Forms of headings. Namely:
Chapter 22	For names of persons.
Chapter 23	For geographic names when they appear in headings.
Chapter 24	For names of corporate bodies – organizations, etc.
Chapter 25	For uniform titles.
Chapter 26	References.

We may now proceed to p.11, to the beginning of the algorithms themselves.

Selective list of further readings

Ayres, F.H. 'Main entry: lynch pin or dodo'. *Journal of Librarianship* **10**(3) July 1978. 170-181

Bakewell, K.G.B. *A manual of cataloguing practice.* Oxford, Pergamon Press 1972. 1-13; 25-69

Downing, Joel. 'Anniversary and birth: AA1908 to AACR2'. *Library Association Record* **8**(2) February 1979. 66-7.

Gorman, Michael. 'The Anglo-American Cataloguing Rules. Second edition.' *Library Resources and Technical Services* **22**(3) Summer 1978. 209-25.

Hunter, Eric and Fox, Nicholas. *Examples illustrating AACR2.* London, Library Association, 1980.

Needham, C.D. *Organizing knowledge in libraries: an introduction to information retrieval.* 2nd rev. ed. London, Andre Deutsch. 11-88.

General introduction to the algorithms

The organization of the rules in Part II of AACR2 reflects the order in which decisions must be taken in the cataloguing process. The cataloguer must:

- Firstly determine what entries (or access points) it is desirable to provide for a document; including the decision on main entry heading if the cataloguing policy of the institution concerned is to make a distinction between 'main' and 'added' entries.
  These decisions are covered by Algorithm 1.
- Secondly, establish the *form* which the headings for those entries will take — whether the heading is the name of a person, the name of an organization, or a title.
  These decisions are covered by Algorithm 2.

Before beginning to work through the algorithms the following points should be carefully noted.

(1) The algorithms will occasionally refer to the 'chief source of information' for a document. This is the part of the document whence the data for cataloguing the item is normally drawn, e.g. the title page of a book. It is specified for each form of material at the beginning of each of the special chapters (2-12) in Part I of the Rules.

(2) The text of the algorithms will normally give a summary of the solution prescribed by the Rules. However, the algorithms should not be regarded as a substitute for the Rules themselves. It will usually be preferable to check the terms of the rules in AACR2 itself (where the examples provided will also be helpful): the appropriate rule numbers are signalled at decision points in the algorithm. In a few cases where the provisions of a ruling are too complex to be expressed in the algorithm you will simply be referred to the appropriate rule number.

(3) The algorithm sometimes indicates specifically the need to provide added entries under alternative access points or references from alternative headings, but generally this is only done when such provision is regarded as being particularly important. The student should be aware, in general, of the directions of the Rules with regard to added entries (Rules 21.29-21.30) and to references (chapter 26): these are not covered directly by the algorithm.

(4) Some decisions may assume that the student is working in the context

of a catalogue. e.g. on p.58, where you are asked to decide 'if there is likely to be confusion between this title and other titles entered under the same heading'. Alternatively, there may be decisions which would be determined by the cataloguing policy of the organization involved, e.g. on p.43 when you must decide whether or not to establish a uniform title. Obviously such decisions can be taken realistically if one is actually working in the context of a catalogue. Otherwise the student should ask the advice of a tutor or take an ad hoc decision.

(5) Occasionally the algorithm may contain an instruction to the effect of 'enter under the heading appropriate for the original work'. This means that you must return to an appropriate point in the algorithm in order to establish that 'appropriate heading'. Sometimes there will be an indication in the algorithm when this is necessary, but there will be instances when the student must recognize the need to do so on his or her own account. *It is vital that the need to do this is recognized: the point being that there may be several levels or stages in the solving of a problem.*

(6) Make your decisions systematically by adhering strictly to the progression of the algorithm. Do not omit stages, and do not 'guess' your decisions.

(7) Do not be deterred by the apparent complexity of some of the pages: you are concerned in following only *one* of the strands on the flow chart.

(8) Make notes of your decisions as you go along. Firstly of the access points which you decide are necessary as you work through Algorithm 1, and then of the elements of headings as you establish them in progressing through Algorithm 2.

(9) Finally, it is important to be aware of the decisions that you are making, and that you do not merely follow the algorithm blindly.

Now, using the first of the examples provided in the text (on p.133) or an item of your own choice, go to the beginning of Algorithm 1 on p.13.

Algorithm 1: Access points

A comparatively rare occurrence is that the title and/or author of a document may have changed, either between *editions* of the work or between *parts* of a work which is in more than one physical part. It is necessary, at the outset, to check this possibility.

NOTE:
(1) A 'title proper' is defined by AACR2 as 'the chief name of an item, including any alternative title but excluding parallel titles and other title information'.
(2) A title proper is deemed to have changed if:
    (a) any change occurs in the first five words (other than an initial article in the nominative case), or
    (b) any important words (nouns, proper names, or initials standing for proper names, adjectives, etc.) are added, deleted, or changed (including changes in spelling), or
    (c) there is any change in the order of words.

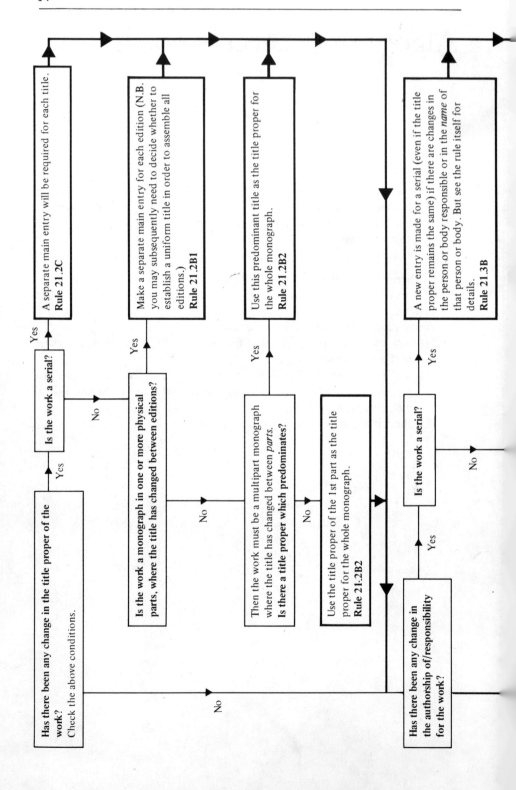

Has there been any change in the title proper of the work?
Check the above conditions.

Is the work a serial?

Yes → A separate main entry will be required for each title. **Rule 21.2C**

No ↓

Is the work a monograph in one or more physical parts, where the title has changed between editions?

Yes → Make a separate main entry for each edition (N.B. you may subsequently need to decide whether to establish a uniform title in order to assemble all editions.) **Rule 21.2B1**

No ↓

Then the work must be a multipart monograph where the title has changed between *parts*. **Is there a title proper which predominates?**

Yes → Use this predominant title as the title proper for the whole monograph. **Rule 21.2B2**

No ↓

Use the title proper of the 1st part as the title proper for the whole monograph. **Rule 21.2B2**

Has there been any change in the authorship of/responsibility for the work?

Yes ↑

Is the work a serial?

Yes → A new entry is made for a serial (even if the title proper remains the same) if there are changes in the person or body responsible or in the *name* of that person or body. But see the rule itself for details. **Rule 21.3B**

No →

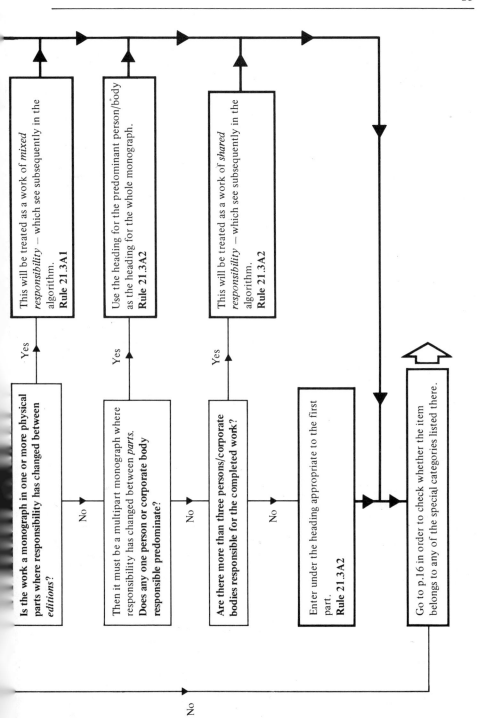

Is the work a monograph in one or more physical parts where responsibility has changed between editions?

Yes → This will be treated as a work of *mixed responsibility* – which see subsequently in the algorithm. **Rule 21.3A1**

No ↓

Then it must be a multipart monograph where responsibility has changed between *parts*. **Does any one person or corporate body responsible predominate?**

Yes → Use the heading for the predominant person/body as the heading for the whole monograph. **Rule 21.3A2**

No ↓

Are there more than three persons/corporate bodies responsible for the completed work?

Yes → This will be treated as a work of *shared responsibility* – which see subsequently in the algorithm. **Rule 21.3A2**

No ↓

Enter under the heading appropriate to the first part. **Rule 21.3A2**

Go to p.16 in order to check whether the item belongs to any of the special categories listed there.

No

The next question is to single out certain special categories of publications which present particular problems to the cataloguer:
(Note: serial publications are no longer treated as special categories.)

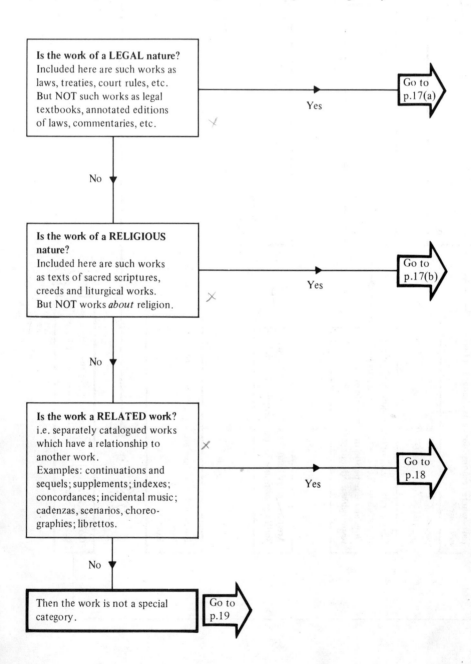

Is the work of a LEGAL nature?
Included here are such works as laws, treaties, court rules, etc. But NOT such works as legal textbooks, annotated editions of laws, commentaries, etc.

Yes → Go to p.17(a)

No ↓

Is the work of a RELIGIOUS nature?
Included here are such works as texts of sacred scriptures, creeds and liturgical works. But NOT works *about* religion.

Yes → Go to p.17(b)

No ↓

Is the work a RELATED work?
i.e. separately catalogued works which have a relationship to another work.
Examples: continuations and sequels; supplements; indexes; concordances; incidental music; cadenzas, scenarios, choreographies; librettos.

Yes → Go to p.18

No ↓

Then the work is not a special category.

Go to p.19

(a) You have arrived here by deciding that:
The work is of a LEGAL nature.

This category of document is NOT covered by the algorithm, as the decisions may be more conveniently made by referring directly to the rules. Select the appropriate heading below, and refer directly to the rule stated.

Laws	21.31
Administrative regulations	21.32
Constitutions and charters	21.33
Court rules	21.34
Treaties and intergovernmental agreement	21.35
Court decisions and cases	21.36

(b) You have arrived here by deciding that:
The work is of a RELIGIOUS nature

This category of document is NOT covered by the algorithm, as the decisions may be more conveniently made by referring directly to the rules. Select the appropriate heading below, and refer directly to the rule stated.

Sacred scriptures	21.37
Creeds and confessions of faith	21.38
Liturgical works	21.39

You have arrived here by deciding that:
The work is RELATED to another work.

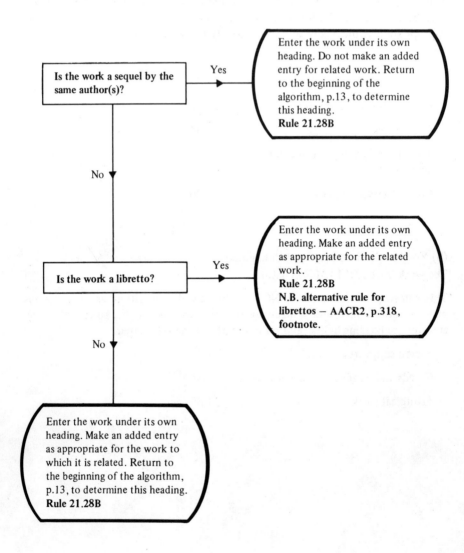

Is the work a sequel by the same author(s)?

Yes

Enter the work under its own heading. Do not make an added entry for related work. Return to the beginning of the algorithm, p.13, to determine this heading.
Rule 21.28B

No

Is the work a libretto?

Yes

Enter the work under its own heading. Make an added entry as appropriate for the related work.
Rule 21.28B
N.B. alternative rule for librettos — AACR2, p.318, footnote.

No

Enter the work under its own heading. Make an added entry as appropriate for the work to which it is related. Return to the beginning of the algorithm, p.13, to determine this heading.
Rule 21.28B

You have arrived here, having explored changes in author and/or title, and having decided that either:

(1) The work does not belong to the special categories listed on p.16

or

(2) The work is a related work and requires entry under its own heading.

You must now decide the nature of the authorship of the document, e.g. single authorship, unknown authorship, shared authorship etc.

Before beginning to work through the algorithm, read the following notes carefully.

Two basic terms require definition:

Author (personal author) — the person chiefly responsible for the creation of the intellectual or artistic content of a work, e.g. writers of books, composers of music.

Corporate body — any organization or group of persons that is identified by a particular name and that acts, or may act, as an entity. Typical examples of corporate bodies are associations, institutions, business firms, non-profit enterprises, governments, government agencies, religious bodies, local churches and conferences.

In certain cases, corporate bodies may be regarded as being responsible for the creation of documents. In such cases the main entry will be made under the appropriate heading for the corporate body. This will apply if the document falls into one or more of the following categories:

(1) Those of an administrative nature dealing with the corporate body itself; its internal policies, procedures, operations; its finances; its officers or staff; its resources (e.g. catalogues, membership directories, etc.).
(2) Some legal and governmental works. See Rule 21.1B2 for the list of types and refer to Rules 21.31; 21.32; 21.35 or 21.36 as necessary.
(3) Those that record the collective thought of the body (e.g. reports of commissions).
(4) Those which report the collective activity of a conference (e.g. proceedings), of an expedition (e.g. results of exploration) or of an event (e.g. an exhibition) instigated by a corporate body, provided that the conference, expedition, or event is prominently named in the item being catalogued.
(5) Sound recordings, films, and videorecordings resulting from the collective activity of a performing group as a whole where the responsibility of the group goes beyond that of mere performance, execution, etc.

Now select the appropriate authorship condition from below. Consider each carefully in the order in which they occur.

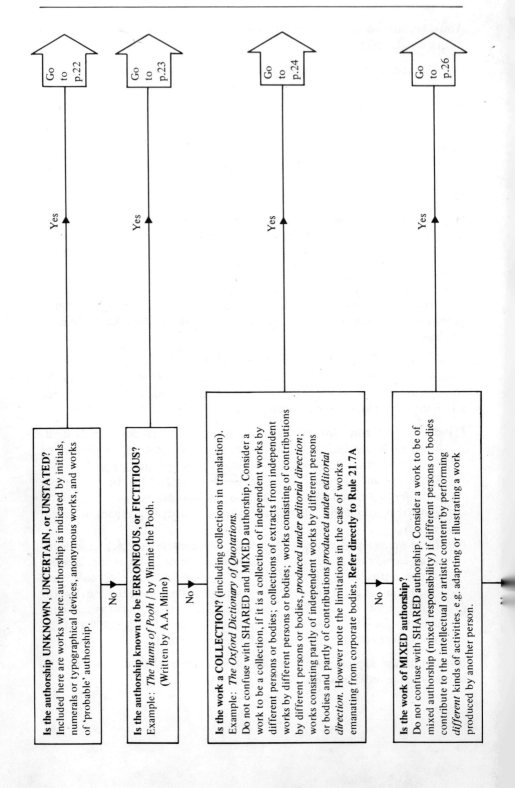

Is the authorship UNKNOWN, UNCERTAIN, or UNSTATED?
Included here are works where authorship is indicated by initials, numerals or typographical devices, anonymous works, and works of 'probable' authorship.

No

Is the authorship known to be ERRONEOUS, or FICTITIOUS?
Example: *The hums of Pooh* / by Winnie the Pooh.
(Written by A.A. Milne)

No

Is the work a COLLECTION? (including collections in translation).
Example: *The Oxford Dictionary of Quotations.*
Do not confuse with SHARED and MIXED authorship. Consider a work to be a collection, if it is a collection of independent works by different persons or bodies; collections of extracts from independent works by different persons or bodies; works consisting of contributions by different persons or bodies, *produced under editorial direction*; works consisting partly of independent works by different persons or bodies and partly of contributions *produced under editorial direction*. However note the limitations in the case of works emanating from corporate bodies. **Refer directly to Rule 21.7A**

No

Is the work of MIXED authorship?
Do not confuse with SHARED authorship. Consider a work to be of mixed authorship (mixed responsibility) if different persons or bodies contribute to the intellectual or artistic content by performing *different* kinds of activities, e.g. adapting or illustrating a work produced by another person.

Yes → Go to p.22

Yes → Go to p.23

Yes → Go to p.24

Yes → Go to p.26

Is the work of SHARED authorship?

i.e. a work produced in collaboration between two or more persons or bodies performing the *same* kind of activity in the creation of the content of a work. The contribution of each collaborator may — or may not — be separate and distinct.

A work is regarded as shared responsibility if it is:

(1) a work produced by the collaboration of two or more persons;

(2) a work for which different persons have prepared separate contributions;

(3) a work consisting of an exchange between two or more persons (e.g. a debate, correspondence etc.);

(4) works *falling into one or more of the types listed on page 19* that emanate from two or more corporate bodies;

(5) works listed in 1-3 above that also contain contributions emanating from one or more corporate bodies;

(6) works resulting from a *collaboration* or exchange between a person and a corporate body. N.B. More than merely the association of both personal and corporate names with a document.

Yes → Go to p.39

No →

Then the work must be a case of SINGLE personal authorship, or emanate from a SINGLE corporate body.

EXCLUDED are works that emanate from a single corporate body but that fall outside the categories listed on p.19. These should be treated as if no corporate body were involved. **Rule 21.1B3**. (Note that if this is so, and no personal authorship is indicated, you will enter under title. **Rule 21.1C(3)**).

In case of doubt whether a work falls into the categories listed on p.19, treat it as if it did not. **Rule 21.1B2**

Go to p.40

You have arrived here by deciding that:
The work is of UNKNOWN, UNCERTAIN or UNSTATED authorship.

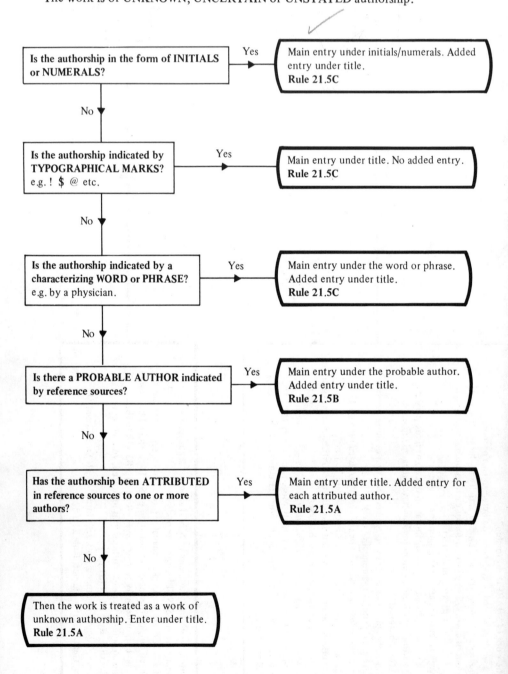

Is the authorship in the form of INITIALS or NUMERALS? — Yes → Main entry under initials/numerals. Added entry under title. **Rule 21.5C**

No ↓

Is the authorship indicated by TYPOGRAPHICAL MARKS? e.g. ! $ @ etc. — Yes → Main entry under title. No added entry. **Rule 21.5C**

No ↓

Is the authorship indicated by a characterizing WORD or PHRASE? e.g. by a physician. — Yes → Main entry under the word or phrase. Added entry under title. **Rule 21.5C**

No ↓

Is there a PROBABLE AUTHOR indicated by reference sources? — Yes → Main entry under the probable author. Added entry under title. **Rule 21.5B**

No ↓

Has the authorship been ATTRIBUTED in reference sources to one or more authors? — Yes → Main entry under title. Added entry for each attributed author. **Rule 21.5A**

No ↓

Then the work is treated as a work of unknown authorship. Enter under title. **Rule 21.5A**

You have arrived here by deciding that:
The work is of ERRONEOUS or FICTITIOUS authorship.

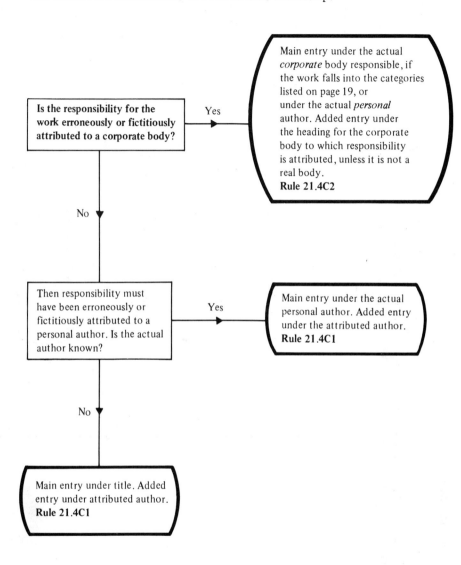

Is the responsibility for the work erroneously or fictitiously attributed to a corporate body?

Yes

Main entry under the actual *corporate* body responsible, if the work falls into the categories listed on page 19, or under the actual *personal* author. Added entry under the heading for the corporate body to which responsibility is attributed, unless it is not a real body.
Rule 21.4C2

No

Then responsibility must have been erroneously or fictitiously attributed to a personal author. Is the actual author known?

Yes

Main entry under the actual personal author. Added entry under the attributed author.
Rule 21.4C1

No

Main entry under title. Added entry under attributed author.
Rule 21.4C1

You have arrived here by deciding that:
The work is a COLLECTION.

Has the work a collective title? — Yes →

Are there three or fewer editors/compilers, named prominently in the work? — Yes →

Are there just two or three contributions or independent works included? — Yes →

Main entry: title.
Added entries: each editor/compiler and name/title for each work.
Rule 21.7B

No →

Are there just two or three contributors involved? — Yes →

Main entry: title.
Added entries: each editor/compiler and each contributor.
Rule 21.7B

No →

Are there more than three contributors named in the chief source of information? — Yes →

Main entry: title.
Added entries: each editor/compiler and first named contributor.
Rule 21.7B

No →

Main entry: title. Added entries: each editor/compiler.
Rule 21.7B

No

No

No

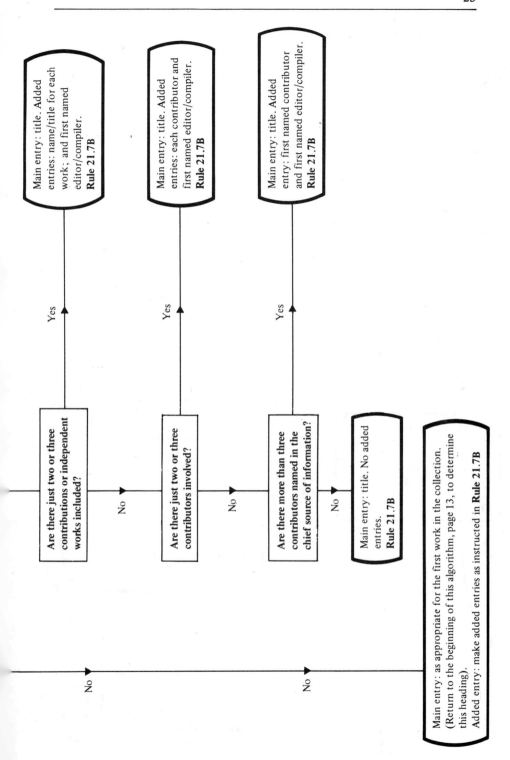

Are there just two or three contributions or independent works included?

Yes → Main entry: title. Added entries: name/title for each work; and first named editor/compiler. **Rule 21.7B**

No ↓

Are there just two or three contributors involved?

Yes → Main entry: title. Added entries: each contributor and first named editor/compiler. **Rule 21.7B**

No ↓

Are there more than three contributors named in the chief source of information?

Yes → Main entry: title. Added entry: first named contributor and first named editor/compiler. **Rule 21.7B**

No → Main entry: title. No added entries. **Rule 21.7B**

Main entry: as appropriate for the first work in the collection. (Return to the beginning of this algorithm, page 13, to determine this heading). Added entry: make added entries as instructed in **Rule 21.7B**

You have arrived here by deciding that:
The authorship is MIXED responsibility.

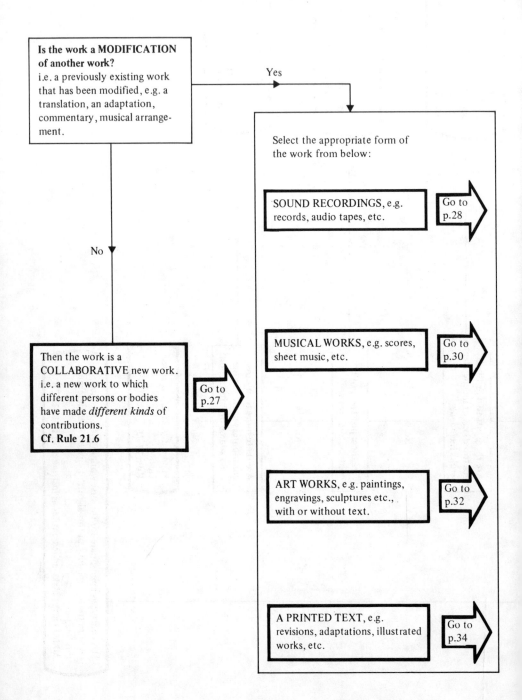

Is the work a MODIFICATION of another work?
i.e. a previously existing work that has been modified, e.g. a translation, an adaptation, commentary, musical arrangement.

Yes

No

Then the work is a COLLABORATIVE new work. i.e. a new work to which different persons or bodies have made *different kinds* of contributions.
Cf. Rule 21.6

Go to p.27

Select the appropriate form of the work from below:

SOUND RECORDINGS, e.g. records, audio tapes, etc.
Go to p.28

MUSICAL WORKS, e.g. scores, sheet music, etc.
Go to p.30

ART WORKS, e.g. paintings, engravings, sculptures etc., with or without text.
Go to p.32

A PRINTED TEXT, e.g. revisions, adaptations, illustrated works, etc.
Go to p.34

You have arrived here by deciding that:
The work is a COLLABORATIVE new work. (N.B. AACR2 treats works consisting of words and music as *modifications of existing works*: see p.34).

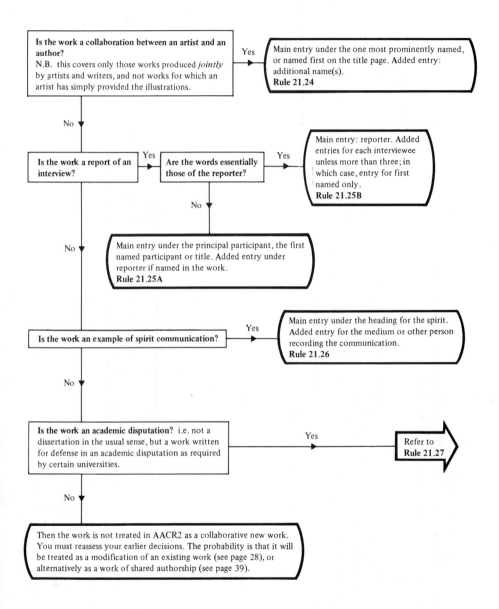

You have arrived here by deciding that:
The authorship is MIXED RESPONSIBILITY and the work is a MODIFICATION of an existing work in the form of a SOUND RECORDING.

Is it a sound recording of a single work, or of two or more works (music, text, etc.), by the same persons?

— Yes →

Are there more than three principal performers? i.e. singers, readers, orchestras etc.

— Yes →

Main entry under appropriate heading for the original work(s). (Return to page 13 to determine this).
Added entry: first named principal performer.
Rule 21.23A

No ↓ (from "more than three principal performers?")

Main entry under appropriate heading for the original work(s). (Return to page 13 to determine this.) Added entry: each principal performer.
Rule 21.23A

No ↓ (from "single work" question)

No ↓

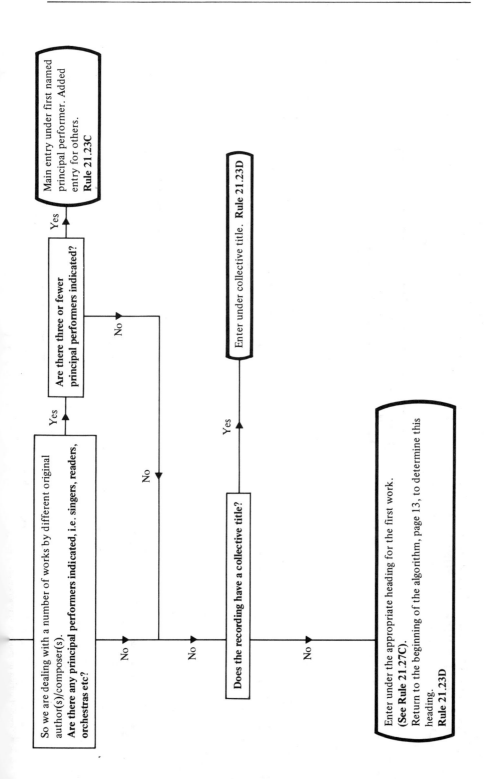

So we are dealing with a number of works by different original author(s)/composer(s).
Are there any principal performers indicated, i.e. singers, readers, orchestras etc?

No →

No →

Does the recording have a collective title?

No →

Yes →

Yes →

Are there three or fewer principal performers indicated?

No →

Yes →

Main entry under first named principal performer. Added entry for others. **Rule 21.23C**

Enter under collective title. **Rule 21.23D**

Enter under the appropriate heading for the first work. **(See Rule 21.27C).**
Return to the beginning of the algorithm, page 13, to determine this heading. **Rule 21.23D**

You have arrived here by deciding that:
The authorship is MIXED RESPONSIBILITY and the work is a MODIFICATION of an existing work in the form of a MUSICAL WORK.

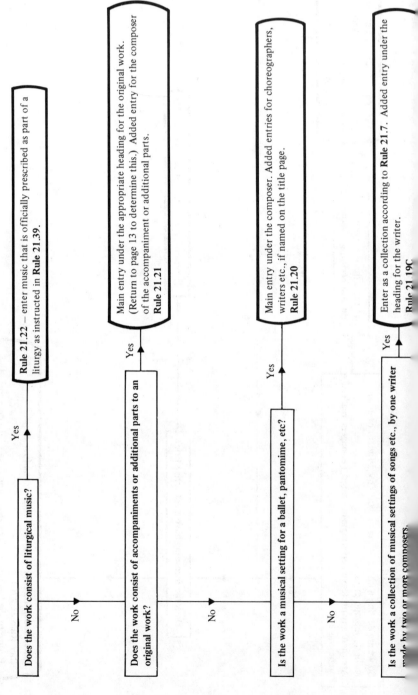

Does the work consist of liturgical music?

Yes → **Rule 21.22** — enter music that is officially prescribed as part of a liturgy as instructed in **Rule 21.39**.

No ↓

Does the work consist of accompaniments or additional parts to an original work?

Yes → Main entry under the appropriate heading for the original work. (Return to page 13 to determine this.) Added entry for the composer of the accompaniment or additional parts. **Rule 21.21**

No ↓

Is the work a musical setting for a ballet, pantomime, etc?

Yes → Main entry under the composer. Added entries for choreographers, writers etc., if named on the title page. **Rule 21.20**

No ↓

Is the work a collection of musical settings of songs etc., by one writer made by two or more composers.

Yes → Enter as a collection according to **Rule 21.7**. Added entry under the heading for the writer. **Rule 21.19C**

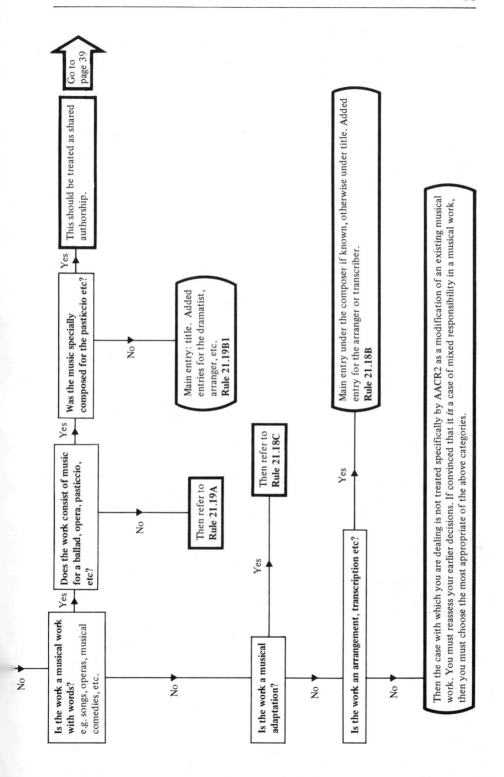

No

Is the work a musical work with words? e.g. songs, operas, musical comedies, etc.

Yes → **Does the work consist of music for a ballad, opera, pasticcio, etc?**

Yes → **Was the music specially composed for the pasticcio etc?**

Yes → This should be treated as shared authorship.

Go to page 39

No → Main entry: title. Added entries for the dramatist, arranger, etc. **Rule 21.19B1**

No → Then refer to **Rule 21.19A**

No

Is the work a musical adaptation?

Yes → Then refer to **Rule 21.18C**

No

Is the work an arrangement, transcription etc?

Yes → Main entry under the composer if known, otherwise under title. Added entry for the arranger or transcriber. **Rule 21.18B**

No → Then the case with which you are dealing is not treated specifically by AACR2 as a modification of an existing musical work. You must reassess your earlier decisions. If convinced that it *is* a case of mixed responsibility in a musical work, then you must choose the most appropriate of the above categories.

You have arrived here by deciding that:

The authorship is MIXED RESPONSIBILITY and the work is a MODIFICATION of an existing work in the form of an ART WORK.

(N.B. collections of works by *different* artists will be treated *as* collections. See page 24).

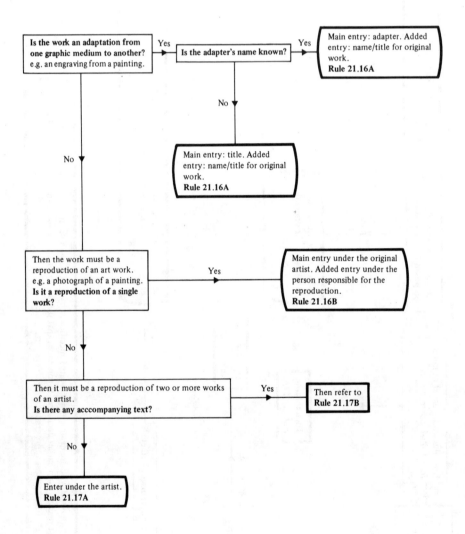

Is the work an adaptation from one graphic medium to another? e.g. an engraving from a painting.

Yes → Is the adapter's name known?

Yes → Main entry: adapter. Added entry: name/title for original work. **Rule 21.16A**

No ↓

Main entry: title. Added entry: name/title for original work. **Rule 21.16A**

No ↓

Then the work must be a reproduction of an art work. e.g. a photograph of a painting. **Is it a reproduction of a single work?**

Yes → Main entry under the original artist. Added entry under the person responsible for the reproduction. **Rule 21.16B**

No ↓

Then it must be a reproduction of two or more works of an artist. **Is there any acccompanying text?**

Yes → Then refer to **Rule 21.17B**

No ↓

Enter under the artist. **Rule 21.17A**

You have arrived here by deciding that:

The work is of MIXED RESPONSIBILITY and is a MODIFICATION of an existing work in the form of an ILLUSTRATED TEXT.

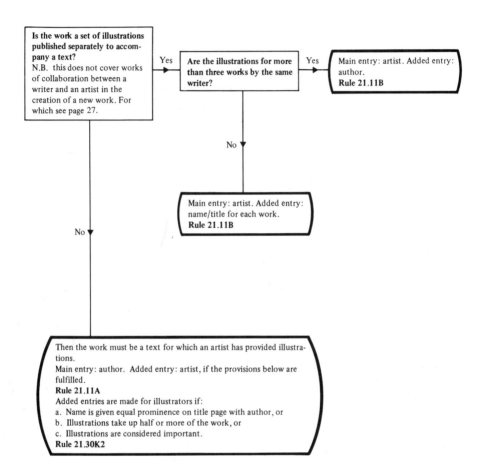

Is the work a set of illustrations published separately to accompany a text?
N.B. this does not cover works of collaboration between a writer and an artist in the creation of a new work. For which see page 27.

Yes →

Are the illustrations for more than three works by the same writer?

Yes →

Main entry: artist. Added entry: author.
Rule 21.11B

No ▼

Main entry: artist. Added entry: name/title for each work.
Rule 21.11B

No ▼

Then the work must be a text for which an artist has provided illustrations.
Main entry: author. Added entry: artist, if the provisions below are fulfilled.
Rule 21.11A
Added entries are made for illustrators if:
a. Name is given equal prominence on title page with author, or
b. Illustrations take up half or more of the work, or
c. Illustrations are considered important.
Rule 21.30K2

You have arrived here by deciding that:

The work is of **MIXED RESPONSIBILITY** and is a **MODIFICATION** of an existing work in the form of a **PRINTED TEXT**.

Select from below:

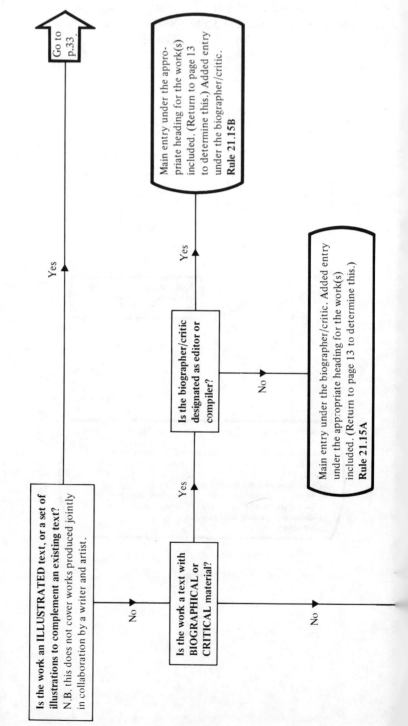

Is the work an **ILLUSTRATED** text, or a set of illustrations to complement an existing text?
N.B. this does not cover works produced jointly in collaboration by a writer and artist.

Yes → Go to p.33.

No ↓

Is the work a text with **BIOGRAPHICAL** or **CRITICAL** material?

Yes →

Is the biographer/critic designated as editor or compiler?

Yes → Main entry under the appropriate heading for the work(s) included. (Return to page 13 to determine this.) Added entry under the biographer/critic. **Rule 21.15B**

No → Main entry under the biographer/critic. Added entry under the appropriate heading for the work(s) included. (Return to page 13 to determine this.) **Rule 21.15A**

No ↓

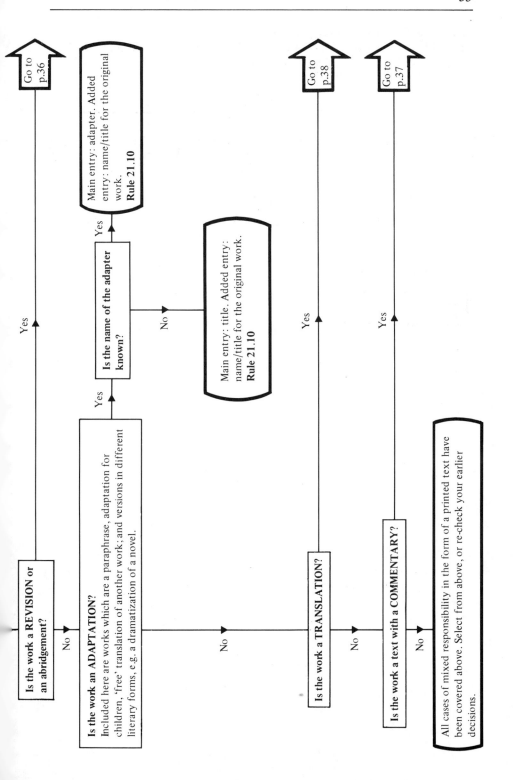

Is the work a REVISION or an abridgement?

Yes → Go to p.36

No ↓

Is the work an ADAPTATION?
Included here are works which are a paraphrase, adaptation for children, 'free' translation of another work; and versions in different literary forms, e.g. a dramatization of a novel.

Yes → **Is the name of the adapter known?**

Yes → Main entry: adapter. Added entry: name/title for the original work. **Rule 21.10**

No → Main entry: title. Added entry: name/title for the original work. **Rule 21.10**

No ↓

Is the work a TRANSLATION?

Yes → Go to p.38

No ↓

Is the work a text with a COMMENTARY?

Yes → Go to p.37

No ↓

All cases of mixed responsibility in the form of a printed text have been covered above. Select from above, or re-check your earlier decisions.

You have arrived here by deciding that:
The work is of MIXED RESPONSIBILITY and is a MODIFICATION of an existing work in the form of a REVISED TEXT.

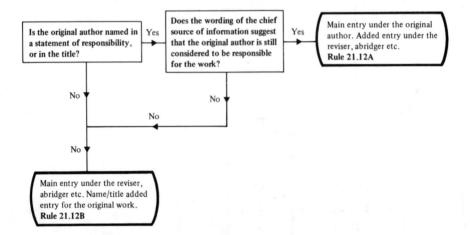

Is the original author named in a statement of responsibility, or in the title? — Yes → Does the wording of the chief source of information suggest that the original author is still considered to be responsible for the work? — Yes → Main entry under the original author. Added entry under the reviser, abridger etc. **Rule 21.12A**

No → No → No

Main entry under the reviser, abridger etc. Name/title added entry for the original work. **Rule 21.12B**

You have arrived here by deciding that:
The work is of MIXED RESPONSIBILITY and is a MODIFICATION of an existing work in the form of a TEXT with COMMENTARY.

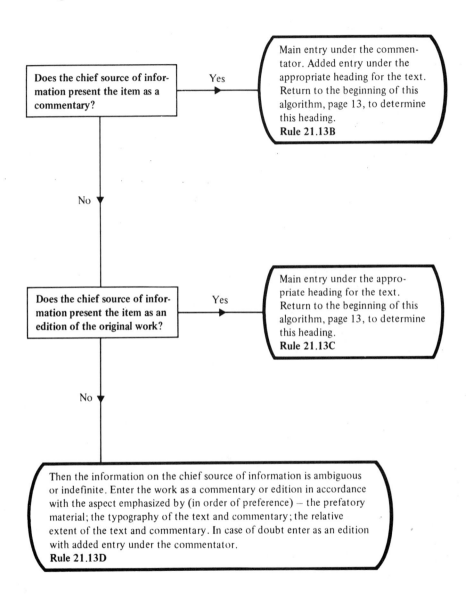

Does the chief source of information present the item as a commentary?

Yes →

Main entry under the commentator. Added entry under the appropriate heading for the text. Return to the beginning of this algorithm, page 13, to determine this heading.
Rule 21.13B

No ↓

Does the chief source of information present the item as an edition of the original work?

Yes →

Main entry under the appropriate heading for the text. Return to the beginning of this algorithm, page 13, to determine this heading.
Rule 21.13C

No ↓

Then the information on the chief source of information is ambiguous or indefinite. Enter the work as a commentary or edition in accordance with the aspect emphasized by (in order of preference) – the prefatory material; the typography of the text and commentary; the relative extent of the text and commentary. In case of doubt enter as an edition with added entry under the commentator.
Rule 21.13D

You have arrived here by deciding that:

The work is of **MIXED RESPONSIBILITY** and is a **MODIFICATION** of an existing work in the form of a **TRANSLATED TEXT**.

> Main entry under the appropriate heading for the original work.
> Return to the beginning of this algorithm, page 13, to determine this heading.
> Added entry under the translator if the provisions below are fulfilled.
> **Rule 21.14A**

Added entry is made for the translator if the main entry heading is for a corporate body or under title. When the main entry is a personal author, an added entry is made for the translator if:

(a) The translation is in verse, or

(b) Important in its own right, or

(c) The work has been translated into the same language more than once, or

(d) The wording of the chief source of information suggests the translator is the author, or

(e) The main entry heading may be difficult for readers to find, (e.g. as with oriental or mediaeval works).

Rule 21.30K1

You have arrived here by deciding that:
The work is of SHARED RESPONSIBILITY.

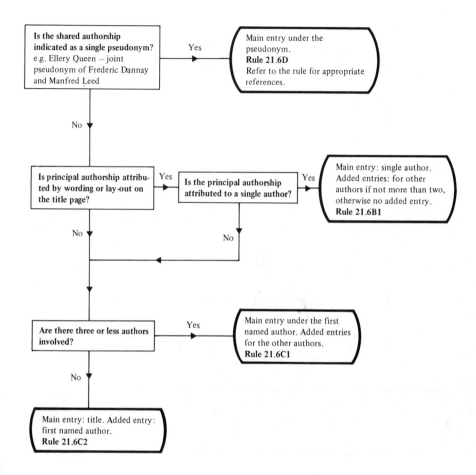

Is the shared authorship indicated as a single pseudonym? e.g. Ellery Queen — joint pseudonym of Frederic Dannay and Manfred Leed

Yes → Main entry under the pseudonym. **Rule 21.6D** Refer to the rule for appropriate references.

No ↓

Is principal authorship attributed by wording or lay-out on the title page?

Yes → Is the principal authorship attributed to a single author?

Yes → Main entry: single author. Added entries: for other authors if not more than two, otherwise no added entry. **Rule 21.6B1**

No ↓

No ↓

Are there three or less authors involved?

Yes → Main entry under the first named author. Added entries for the other authors. **Rule 21.6C1**

No ↓

Main entry: title. Added entry: first named author. **Rule 21.6C2**

You have arrived here by deciding that:
The work is of SINGLE personal authorship, or emanates from a SINGLE corporate body.

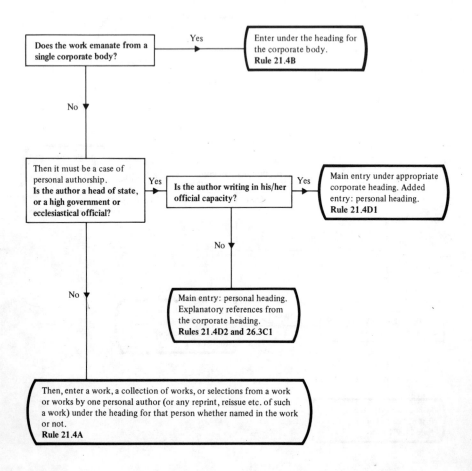

Does the work emanate from a single corporate body?

Yes → Enter under the heading for the corporate body.
Rule 21.4B

No ↓

Then it must be a case of personal authorship.
Is the author a head of state, or a high government or ecclesiastical official?

Yes → Is the author writing in his/her official capacity?

Yes → Main entry under appropriate corporate heading. Added entry: personal heading.
Rule 21.4D1

No ↓

Main entry: personal heading. Explanatory references from the corporate heading.
Rules 21.4D2 and 26.3C1

No ↓

Then, enter a work, a collection of works, or selections from a work or works by one personal author (or any reprint, reissue etc. of such a work) under the heading for that person whether named in the work or not.
Rule 21.4A

Algorithm 2 : Form of heading

You have decided upon the entries or access points required for a document. It will now be necessary to determine the *form* which the headings for these entries will take. There will be a main entry and, usually, a number of added entries. It may also be necessary to provide references from discounted forms of headings to the preferred forms. e.g. A main entry under the name of a personal author, with added entries under the name of a corporate body in some way associated with the document and under its title. Consequently you may need to check, ultimately, more than one of the following strands.

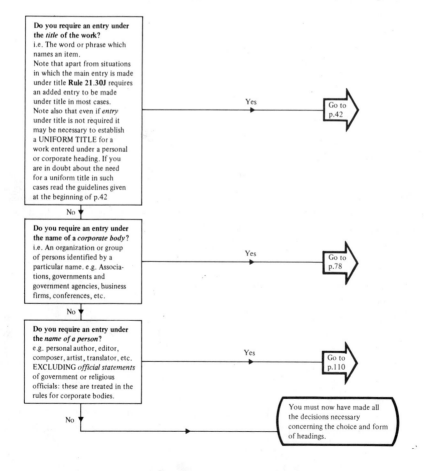

Do you require an entry under the *title* of the work?
i.e. The word or phrase which names an item.
Note that apart from situations in which the main entry is made under title **Rule 21.30J** requires an added entry to be made under title in most cases.
Note also that even if *entry* under title is not required it may be necessary to establish a UNIFORM TITLE for a work entered under a personal or corporate heading. If you are in doubt about the need for a uniform title in such cases read the guidelines given at the beginning of p.42

Yes → Go to p.42

No ↓

Do you require an entry under the name of a *corporate body*?
i.e. An organization or group of persons identified by a particular name. e.g. Associations, governments and government agencies, business firms, conferences, etc.

Yes → Go to p.78

No ↓

Do you require an entry under the *name of a person*?
e.g. personal author, editor, composer, artist, translator, etc. EXCLUDING *official statements* of government or religious officials: these are treated in the rules for corporate bodies.

Yes → Go to p.110

No ↓

You must now have made all the decisions necessary concerning the choice and form of headings.

You have arrived here by deciding that an entry under TITLE is required.

If the work being catalogued has appeared at different times under varying titles then it may be necessary to establish a UNIFORM TITLE. i.e. a particular title by which the work may be identified for cataloguing purposes in order to collocate, or bring together, all entries for a particular work under that one form of title rather than distribute entries for that work under a number (possibly a very large number) of different titles. An example would be *The Arabian nights*, which has appeared under very many variant titles in its different editions and versions.

Even if a work is entered under the heading of a personal author or corporate body it may be considered necessary to establish a uniform title.

e.g. Defoe, Daniel
      The life and adventures of Robinson Crusoe . . .

Defoe, Daniel
      The adventures of Robinson Crusoe . . .

These entries might be separated in a sequence of entries under the heading for Defoe.

If a uniform title, say, 'Robinson Crusoe' was to be established it would appear before the title proper in the catalogue entry, and thus collocate entries for the work 'Robinson Crusoe' under the heading for Defoe.

i.e. Defoe, Daniel
      [Robinson Crusoe]
      The life and adventures of Robinson Crusoe . . .

Defoe, Daniel
      [Robinson Crusoe]
      The adventures of Robinson Crusoe . . .

Consequently, chapter 25 of AACR2 — Uniform titles — to which this section of the algorithm relates, considers the creation of uniform titles which may be used as headings *and/or* filing titles under an author heading.

Basic rules for uniform titles

(1) Uniform titles are normally given in square brackets, whether they appear as headings or otherwise.
(2) Titles selected as uniform titles which are in a non-roman script are transliterated according to the transliteration table for the language adopted by the cataloguing agency.
(3) If the main entry for a work is made under a uniform title then an added entry is made under the title proper for the work being catalogued, with references from any other variants of the title.
(4) If the main entry has been made under a personal author or corporate body and a uniform title is used then a name-title reference is made from

variants of the title, with an added entry under the title proper of the work being catalogued. Read Rules 25.1-25.2 for further explanation.

AACR2 recognizes that the need to establish uniform titles may vary from one catalogue to another. In Rule 25.1 guidelines are laid down to assist in determining whether a uniform title should be established. These are:

(a) How well the work is known
(b) How many manifestations of the work are involved
(c) Whether the main entry is under title
(d) The extent to which the catalogue is used for research purposes.

Rule 25.1 goes on to say, 'Although the rules in this chapter are stated as instructions, apply them according to the policy of the cataloguing agency'.

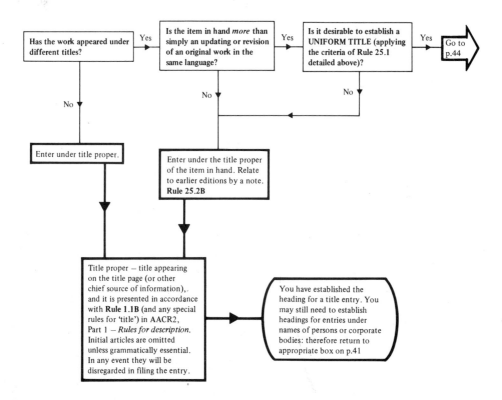

You have arrived here by deciding that: an entry under TITLE is required and that a UNIFORM TITLE SHOULD BE ESTABLISHED.

Uniform titles for certain categories of works require special consideration. Note that more than one of the categories identified below might apply simultaneously in some instances. e.g. one might have a *liturgical work* which is also an *incunabulum*, or a *manuscript group* of *sacred scriptures*. The Rules themselves are not explicit as to the priority which should apply in situations such as these. Our decision has been to impose an order of precedence which follows the order in which the categories are listed below.

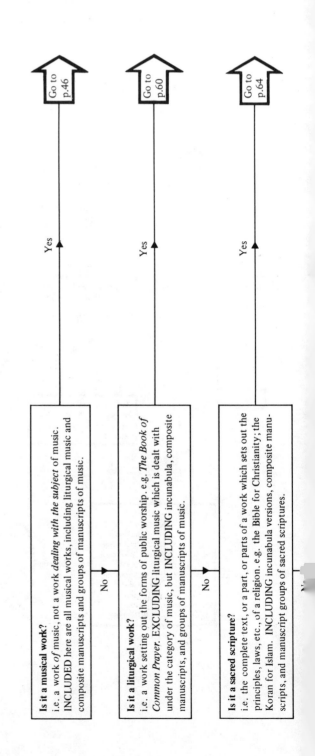

Is it a musical work?
i.e. a work *of* music, not a work *dealing with the subject of* music. INCLUDED here are all musical works, including liturgical music and composite manuscripts and groups of manuscripts of music.

No

Yes — Go to p.46

Is it a liturgical work?
i.e. a work setting out the forms of public worship. e.g. *The Book of Common Prayer*. EXCLUDING liturgical music which is dealt with under the category of music, but INCLUDING incunabula, composite manuscripts, and groups of manuscripts of music.

No

Yes — Go to p.60

Is it a sacred scripture?
i.e. the complete text, or a part, or parts of a work which sets out the principles, laws, etc., of a religion. e.g. the Bible for Christianity; the Koran for Islam. INCLUDING incunabula versions, composite manuscripts, and manuscript groups of sacred scriptures.

Yes — Go to p.64

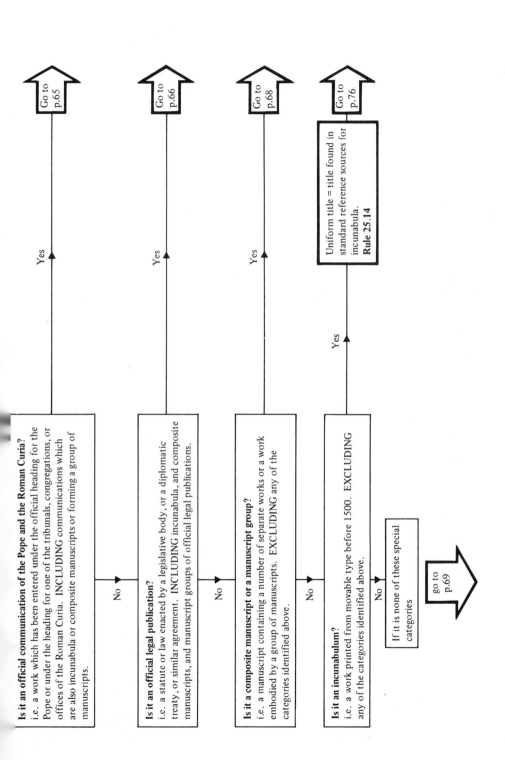

Is it an official communication of the Pope and the Roman Curia?
i.e. a work which has been entered under the official heading for the Pope or under the heading for one of the tribunals, congregations, or offices of the Roman Curia. INCLUDING communications which are also incunabula or composite manuscripts or forming a group of manuscripts.

Yes → Go to p.65

No ↓

Is it an official legal publication?
i.e. a statute or law enacted by a legislative body, or a diplomatic treaty, or similar agreement. INCLUDING incunabula, and composite manuscripts, and manuscript groups of official legal publications.

Yes → Go to p.66

No ↓

Is it a composite manuscript or a manuscript group?
i.e. a manuscript containing a number of separate works or a work embodied by a group of manuscripts. EXCLUDING any of the categories identified above.

Yes → Go to p.68

No ↓

Is it an incunabulum?
i.e. a work printed from movable type before 1500. EXCLUDING any of the categories identified above.

Yes → Uniform title = title found in standard reference sources for incunabula. **Rule 25.14** → Go to p.76

No ↓

If it is none of these special categories → go to p.69

You have arrived here by deciding that:
An entry under TITLE is required, a UNIFORM TITLE should be established and that you are dealing with a MUSICAL WORK (as defined on p.44).

You should begin by examining the definitions given in Rule 25.26 of the terms 'Title' and 'Work' — as they are used in the rules for uniform titles for music. Briefly these state:

Title means the word or words that name the work exclusive of:

(1) a statement of medium of performance
(2) key
(3) serial, opus, or thematic index numbers
(4) numerals (unless they are integral parts of the title)
(5) date of composition
(6) adjectives and epithets not part of the original title of the work.

Work means

(1) a work that is a single unit intended for performance as a whole
(2) a set of works with a group title (not necessarily intended for performance as a whole)
(3) a group of works with a single opus number.

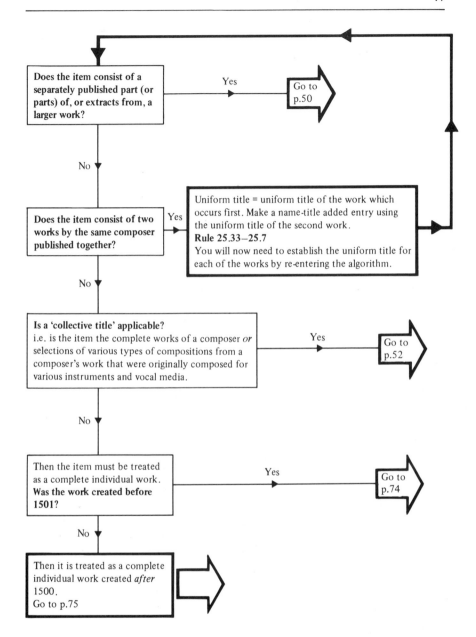

Does the item consist of a separately published part (or parts) of, or extracts from, a larger work?

Yes → Go to p.50

No ↓

Does the item consist of two works by the same composer published together?

Yes → Uniform title = uniform title of the work which occurs first. Make a name-title added entry using the uniform title of the second work.
Rule 25.33–25.7
You will now need to establish the uniform title for each of the works by re-entering the algorithm.

No ↓

Is a 'collective title' applicable?
i.e. is the item the complete works of a composer *or* selections of various types of compositions from a composer's work that were originally composed for various instruments and vocal media.

Yes → Go to p.52

No ↓

Then the item must be treated as a complete individual work.
Was the work created before 1501?

Yes → Go to p.74

No ↓

Then it is treated as a complete individual work created *after* 1500.
Go to p.75

You have arrived here by deciding that:

An entry under TITLE is required, a UNIFORM TITLE should be established and that an INDIVIDUAL MUSICAL WORK is involved. In addition you have established the BASIS for the uniform title. The precise uniform title must now be formulated by applying Rules 25.27–25.36 to this basis.

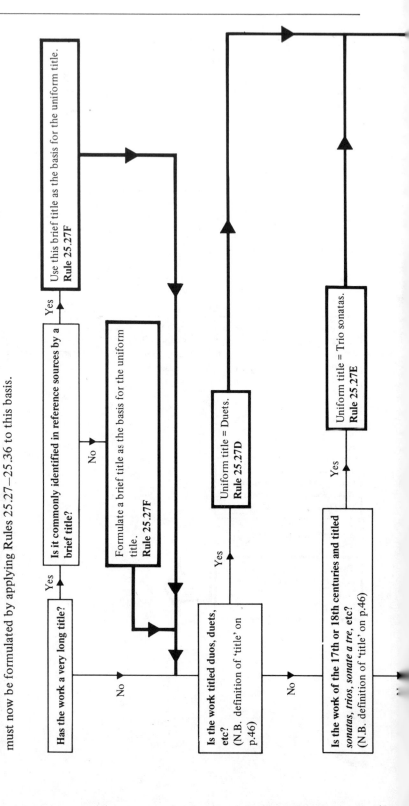

Has the work a very long title?

No →

Yes → **Is it commonly identified in reference sources by a brief title?**

Yes → Use this brief title as the basis for the uniform title. **Rule 25.27F**

No → Formulate a brief title as the basis for the uniform title. **Rule 25.27F**

Is the work titled duos, duets, etc? (N.B. definition of 'title' on p.46)

Yes → Uniform title = Duets. **Rule 25.27D**

No → **Is the work of the 17th or 18th centuries and titled *sonatas, trios, sonate a tre,* etc?** (N.B. definition of 'title' on p.46)

Yes → Uniform title = Trio sonatas. **Rule 25.27E**

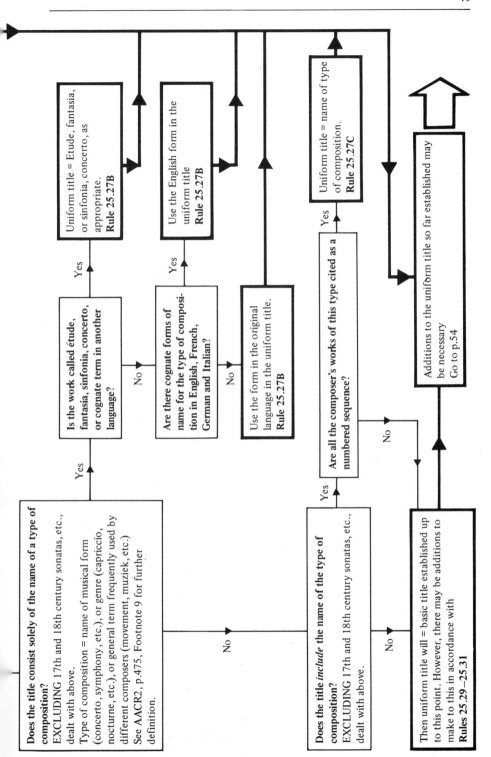

You have arrived here by deciding that:

An entry under TITLE is required, a UNIFORM TITLE should be established and that a PART or PARTS of, or EXTRACTS from, a MUSICAL WORK are involved.

See facing page

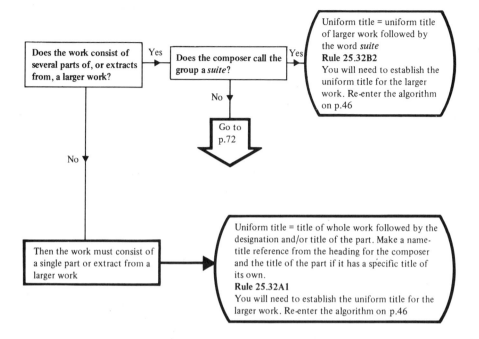

Does the work consist of several parts of, or extracts from, a larger work?

Yes →

Does the composer call the group a *suite*?

Yes →

Uniform title = uniform title of larger work followed by the word *suite*
Rule 25.32B2
You will need to establish the uniform title for the larger work. Re-enter the algorithm on p.46

No ↓

Go to p.72

No ↓

Then the work must consist of a single part or extract from a larger work

→

Uniform title = title of whole work followed by the designation and/or title of the part. Make a name-title reference from the heading for the composer and the title of the part if it has a specific title of its own.
Rule 25.32A1
You will need to establish the uniform title for the larger work. Re-enter the algorithm on p.46

You have arrived here by deciding that:

An entry under TITLE is required, a UNIFORM TITLE should be established, you are dealing with a MUSICAL WORK, and that a COLLECTIVE TITLE (as defined on p.46) is applicable.

Definitions As a preliminary it is necessary to define the way in which two terms are used in the Rules.

(1) *Type of composition* implies name of musical form (concerto, symphony, etc.) or genre (capriccio nocturne, etc.), or a general term used frequently by different composers (movement, muziek, etc.). See AACR2, p.475, Footnote 9 for further definition

(2) *Medium* means medium of performance, both instrumental and vocal. See AACR2, p. 477, Footnote 10 for further definition.

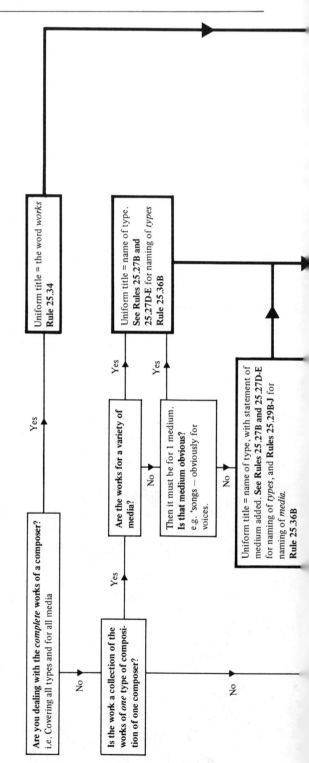

Are you dealing with the *complete* works of a composer?
i.e. Covering all types and for all media

No / Yes

Is the work a collection of the works of *one* type of composition of one composer?

No / Yes

Are the works for a variety of media?

No / Yes

Then it must be for 1 medium.
Is that medium obvious?
e.g. 'songs – obviously for voices.

No / Yes

Uniform title = the word *works*
Rule 25.34

Uniform title = name of type.
See Rules 25.27B and 25.27D-E for naming of *types*
Rule 25.36B

Uniform title = name of type, with statement of medium added. **See Rules 25.27B and 25.27D-E** for naming of *types*, and **Rules 25.29B-J** for naming of *media*.
Rule 25.36B

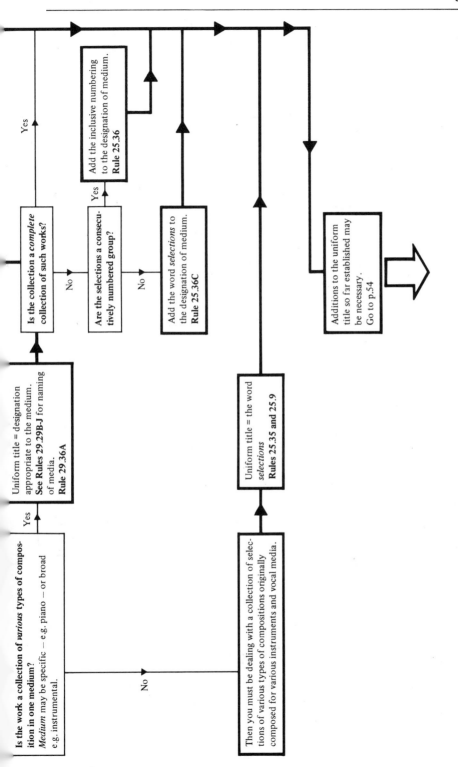

Is the work a collection of *various* types of composition in one medium? *Medium* may be specific — e.g. piano — or broad e.g. instrumental.

Yes → Uniform title = designation appropriate to the medium. See **Rules 29.29B-J** for naming of media. **Rule 29.36A**

Is the collection a *complete* collection of such works?

Yes → Add the inclusive numbering to the designation of medium. **Rule 25.36**

No → **Are the selections a consecutively numbered group?**

Yes → (Add the inclusive numbering to the designation of medium. **Rule 25.36**)

No → Add the word *selections* to the designation of medium. **Rule 25.36C**

No → Then you must be dealing with a collection of selections of various types of compositions originally composed for various instruments and vocal media.

Uniform title = the word *selections* **Rules 25.35 and 25.9**

Additions to the uniform title so far established may be necessary. Go to p.54

You have arrived here by deciding that:
An entry under TITLE is required, a UNIFORM TITLE should be established and that a MUSICAL WORK is involved. You have formulated a basic uniform title and must now decide what ADDITIONS to this title, if any, are necessary.

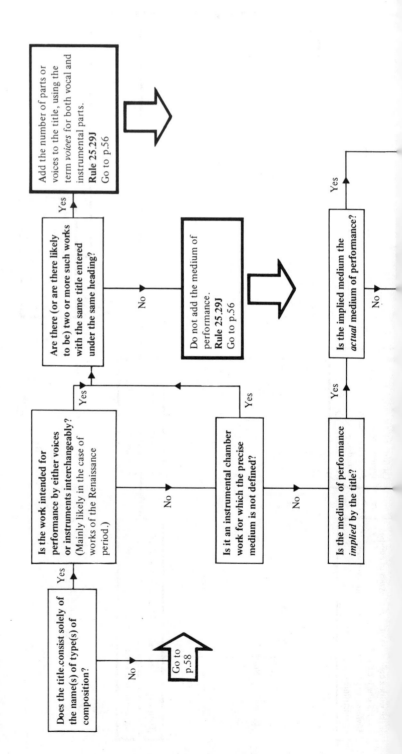

Does the title consist solely of the name(s) of type(s) of composition?

No → Go to p.58

Yes → Is the work intended for performance by either voices or instruments interchangeably? (Mainly likely in the case of works of the Renaissance period.)

No → Is it an instrumental chamber work for which the precise medium is not defined?

Yes →

No → Is the medium of performance *implied* by the title?

Yes → Is the implied medium the *actual* medium of performance?

No →

Yes →

Yes → Are there (or are there likely to be) two or more such works with the same title entered under the same heading?

No → Do not add the medium of performance.
Rule 25.29J
Go to p.56

Yes → Add the number of parts or voices to the title, using the term *voices* for both vocal and instrumental parts.
Rule 25.29J
Go to p.56

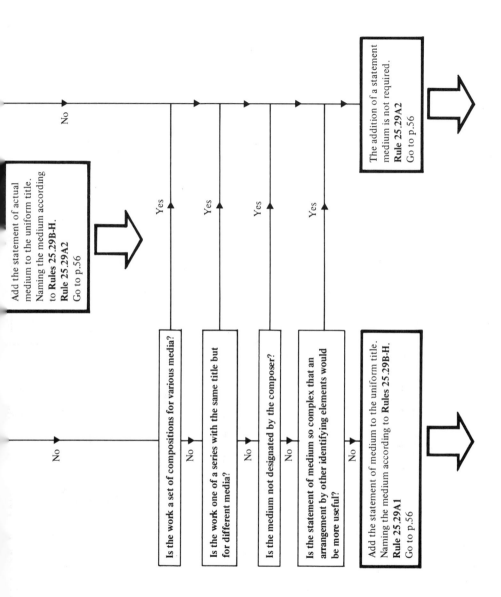

Add the statement of actual medium to the uniform title. Naming the medium according to **Rules 25.29B-H**.
Rule 25.29A2
Go to p.56

No

Yes

Is the work a set of compositions for various media?

No

Is the work one of a series with the same title but for different media?

No

Is the medium not designated by the composer?

No

Is the statement of medium so complex that an arrangement by other identifying elements would be more useful?

No

Yes

Yes

Yes

Add the statement of medium to the uniform title. Naming the medium according to **Rules 25.29B-H**.
Rule 25.29A1
Go to p.56

No

The addition of a statement medium is not required.
Rule 25.29A2
Go to p.56

We are continuing with ADDITIONS to uniform titles for a MUSICAL WORK whose title is SOLELY THE NAME(S) OF A TYPE(S) OF COMPOSITION. You have taken a decision about the addition of medium of performance. You now need to decide about further additions. Any further additions appear in the uniform title in the order in which they occur below.

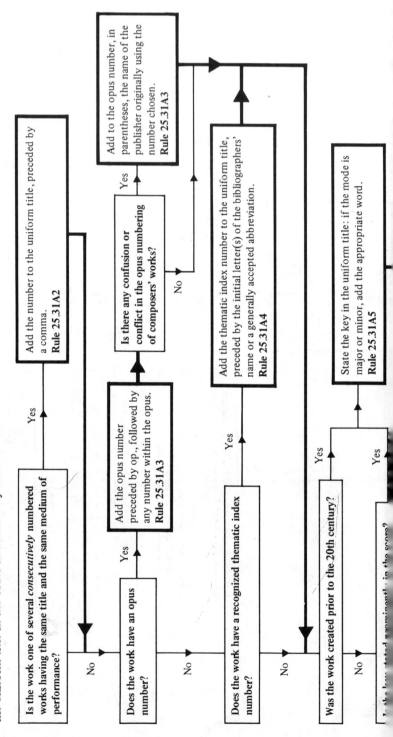

Is the work one of several *consecutively* numbered works having the same title and the same medium of performance?

Yes → Add the number to the uniform title, preceded by a comma. **Rule 25.31A2**

No ↓

Does the work have an opus number?

Yes → Add the opus number preceded by op., followed by any number within the opus. **Rule 25.31A3**

→ **Is there any confusion or conflict in the opus numbering of composers' works?**

Yes → Add to the opus number, in parentheses, the name of the publisher originally using the number chosen. **Rule 25.31A3**

No →

No ↓

Does the work have a recognized thematic index number?

Yes → Add the thematic index number to the uniform title, preceded by the initial letter(s) of the bibliographers' name or a generally accepted abbreviation. **Rule 25.31A4**

No ↓

Was the work created prior to the 20th century?

Yes → State the key in the uniform title: if the mode is major or minor, add the appropriate word. **Rule 25.31A5**

Yes

No ↓

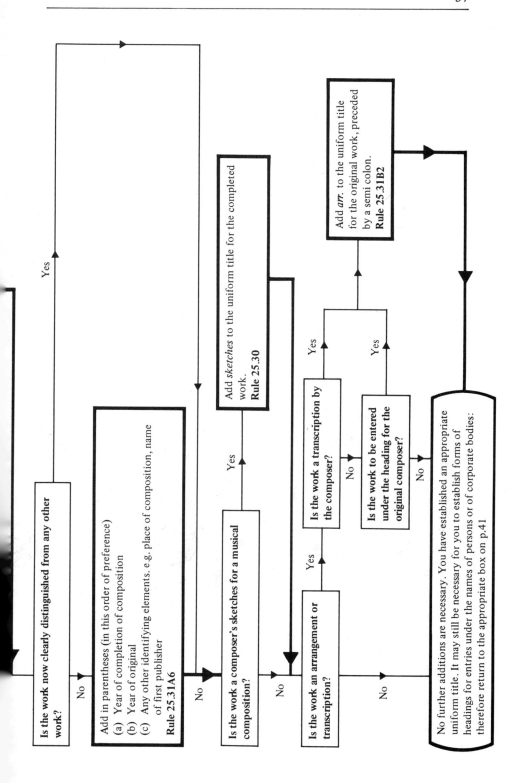

Is the work now clearly distinguished from any other work?

Yes

No

Add in parentheses (in this order of preference)
(a) Year of completion of composition
(b) Year of original
(c) Any other identifying elements. e.g. place of composition, name of first publisher
Rule 25.31A6

Is the work a composer's sketches for a musical composition?

Yes

Add *sketches* to the uniform title for the completed work.
Rule 25.30

No

Is the work an arrangement or transcription?

Yes

No

Is the work a transcription by the composer?

Yes

No

Is the work to be entered under the heading for the original composer?

Yes

No

Add *arr.* to the uniform title for the original work, preceded by a semi colon.
Rule 25.31B2

No further additions are necessary. You have established an appropriate uniform title. It may still be necessary for you to establish forms of headings for entries under the names of persons or of corporate bodies: therefore return to the appropriate box on p.41

You have arrived here having established a UNIFORM TITLE for a MUSICAL WORK and now need to make decisions about ADDITIONS to the uniform title which consists of MORE than solely the name of a type of composition.

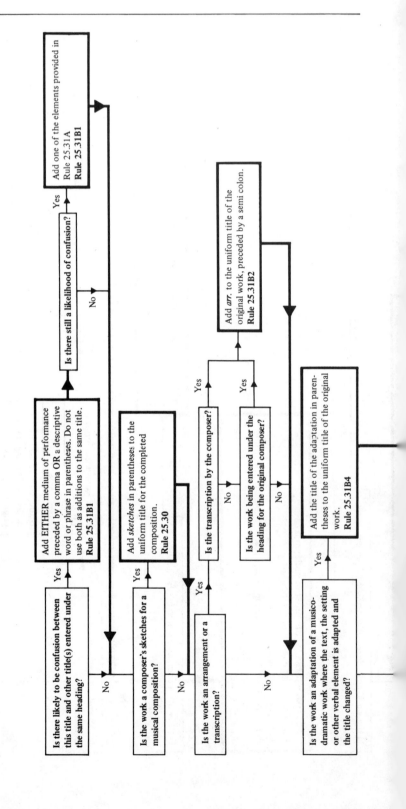

Is there likely to be confusion between this title and other title(s) entered under the same heading?

Yes → Add EITHER medium of performance preceded by a comma OR a descriptive word or phrase in parentheses. Do not use both as additions to the same title. **Rule 25.31B1**

Is there still a likelihood of confusion?

Yes → Add one of the elements provided in Rule 25.31A **Rule 25.31B1**

No

Is the work a composer's sketches for a musical composition?

Yes → Add *sketches* in parentheses to the uniform title for the completed composition. **Rule 25.30**

No

Is the work an arrangement or a transcription?

Yes → Is the transcription by the composer?

No → Is the work being entered under the heading for the original composer?

Yes → Add *arr.* to the uniform title of the original work, preceded by a semi colon. **Rule 25.31B2**

No

Is the work an adaptation of a musico-dramatic work where the text, the setting or other verbal element is adapted and the title changed?

Yes → Add the title of the adaptation in parentheses to the uniform title of the original work. **Rule 25.31B4**

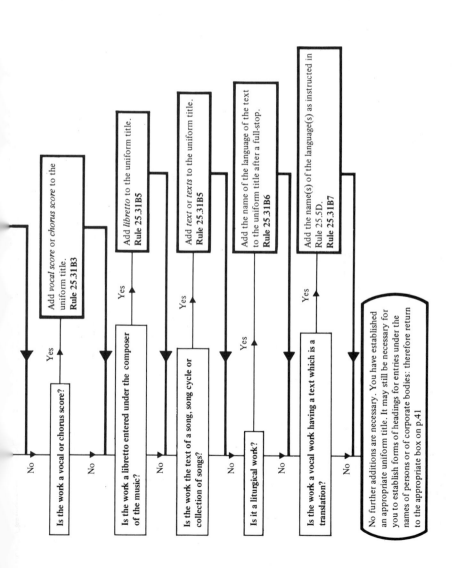

You have arrived here by deciding that:
An entry under TITLE is required, a UNIFORM TITLE should be established
and that a LITURGICAL WORK is involved.

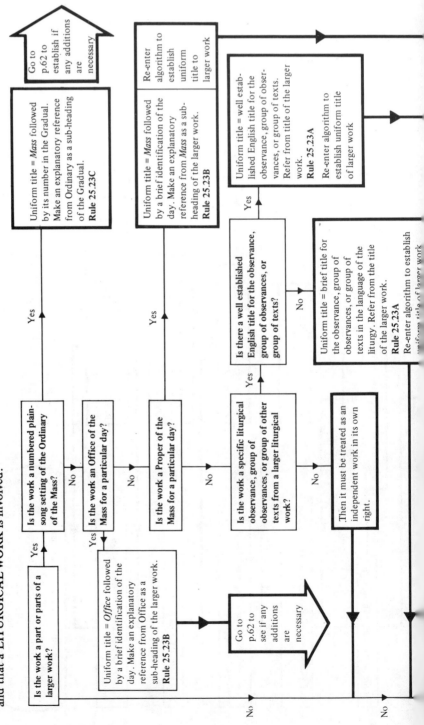

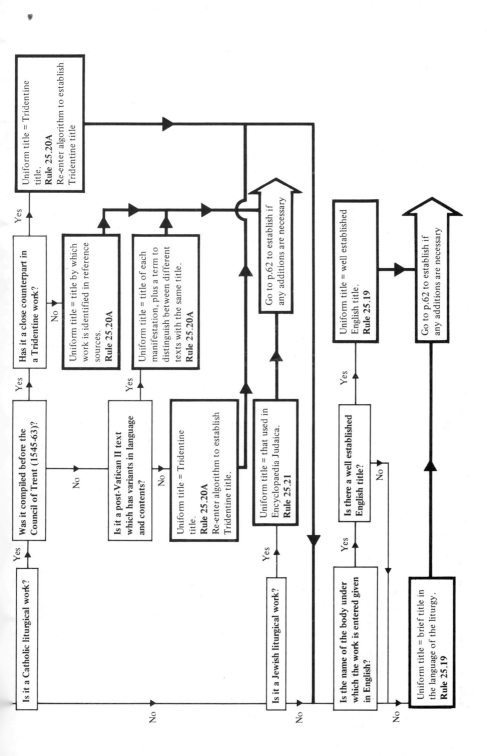

You have established a basic UNIFORM TITLE for a LITURGICAL WORK.
You now need to determine if any ADDITIONS to this basic title are necessary.

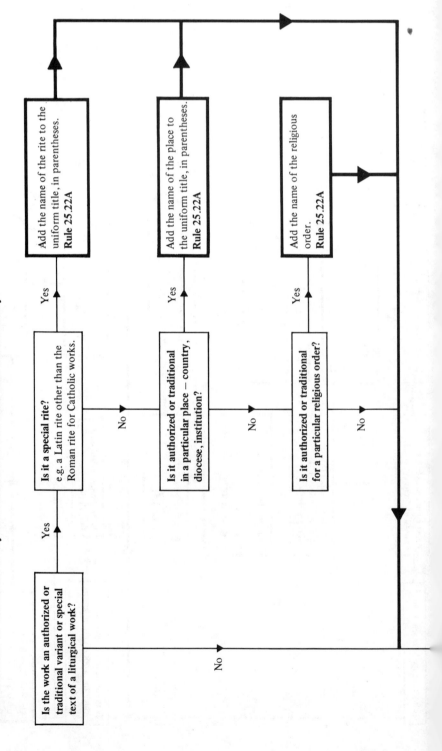

Is the work an authorized or traditional variant or special text of a liturgical work?

Yes →

Is it a special rite?
e.g. a Latin rite other than the Roman rite for Catholic works.

Yes →

Add the name of the rite to the uniform title, in parentheses.
Rule 25.22A

No

Is it authorized or traditional in a particular place — country, diocese, institution?

Yes →

Add the name of the place to the uniform title, in parentheses.
Rule 25.22A

No

Is it authorized or traditional for a particular religious order?

Yes →

Add the name of the religious order.
Rule 25.22A

No

No

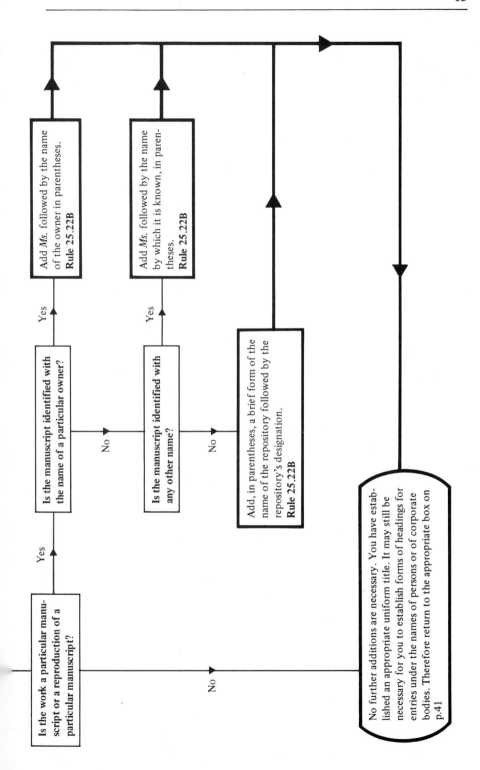

Is the work a particular manuscript or a reproduction of a particular manuscript?

Yes → Is the manuscript identified with the name of a particular owner?

Yes → Add *Ms.* followed by the name of the owner in parentheses. **Rule 25.22B**

No → Is the manuscript identified with any other name?

Yes → Add *Ms.* followed by the name by which it is known, in parentheses. **Rule 25.22B**

No → Add, in parentheses, a brief form of the name of the repository followed by the repository's designation. **Rule 25.22B**

No → No further additions are necessary. You have established an appropriate uniform title. It may still be necessary for you to establish forms of headings for entries under the names of persons or of corporate bodies. Therefore return to the appropriate box on p.41

You have arrived here by deciding that:
An entry under TITLE is required, a UNIFORM TITLE should be established and that the work is the COMPLETE TEXT, a PART, or PARTS of a SACRED SCRIPTURE.

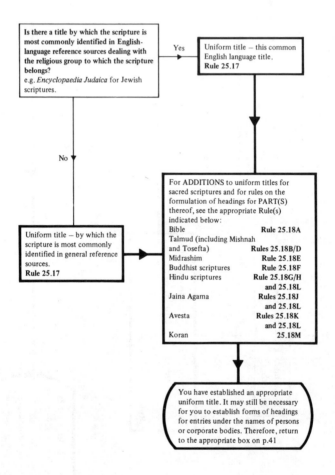

Is there a title by which the scripture is most commonly identified in English-language reference sources dealing with the religious group to which the scripture belongs?
e.g. *Encyclopaedia Judaica* for Jewish scriptures.

Yes

Uniform title – this common English language title.
Rule 25.17

No

Uniform title – by which the scripture is most commonly identified in general reference sources.
Rule 25.17

For ADDITIONS to uniform titles for sacred scriptures and for rules on the formulation of headings for PART(S) thereof, see the appropriate Rule(s) indicated below:

Bible	**Rule 25.18A**
Talmud (including Mishnah and Tosefta)	**Rules 25.18B/D**
Midrashim	**Rule 25.18E**
Buddhist scriptures	**Rule 25.18F**
Hindu scriptures	**Rule 25.18G/H and 25.18L**
Jaina Agama	**Rules 25.18J and 25.18L**
Avesta	**Rules 25.18K and 25.18L**
Koran	**25.18M**

You have established an appropriate uniform title. It may still be necessary for you to establish forms of headings for entries under the names of persons or corporate bodies. Therefore, return to the appropriate box on p.41

You have arrived here by deciding that:
An entry under TITLE is required, a UNIFORM TITLE should be established and that the work is an OFFICIAL PAPAL COMMUNICATION.

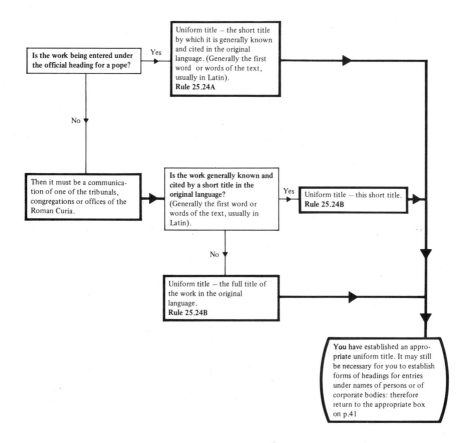

Is the work being entered under the official heading for a pope?

Yes → Uniform title — the short title by which it is generally known and cited in the original language. (Generally the first word or words of the text, usually in Latin).
Rule 25.24A

No ↓

Then it must be a communication of one of the tribunals, congregations or offices of the Roman Curia.

Is the work generally known and cited by a short title in the original language?
(Generally the first word or words of the text, usually in Latin).

Yes → Uniform title — this short title.
Rule 25.24B

No ↓

Uniform title — the full title of the work in the original language.
Rule 25.24B

You have established an appropriate uniform title. It may still be necessary for you to establish forms of headings for entries under names of persons or of corporate bodies: therefore return to the appropriate box on p.41

You have arrived here by deciding that:
An entry under TITLE is required, a UNIFORM TITLE should be established and that the work is an OFFICIAL LEGAL PUBLICATION.

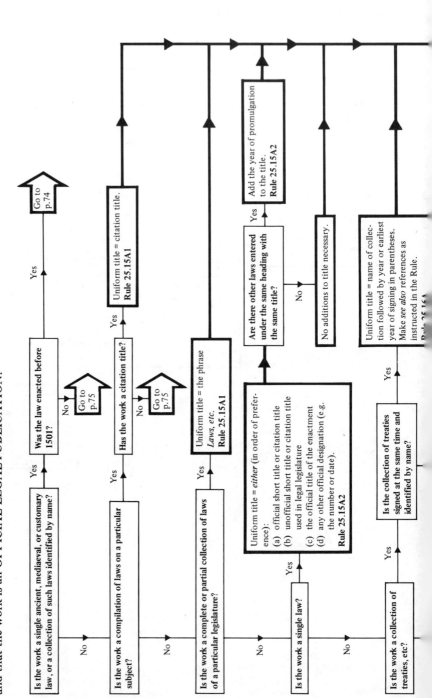

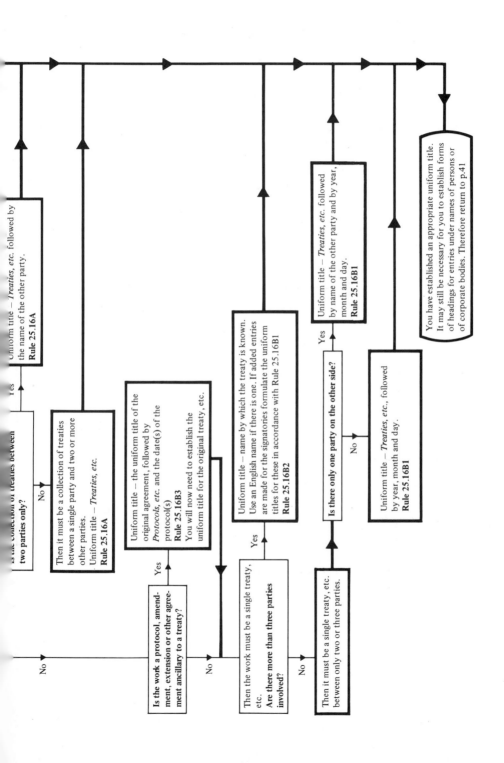

68

You have arrived here by deciding that:
An entry under TITLE is required, a UNIFORM TITLE should be established
and that the work is a COMPOSITE MANUSCRIPT or MANUSCRIPT GROUP

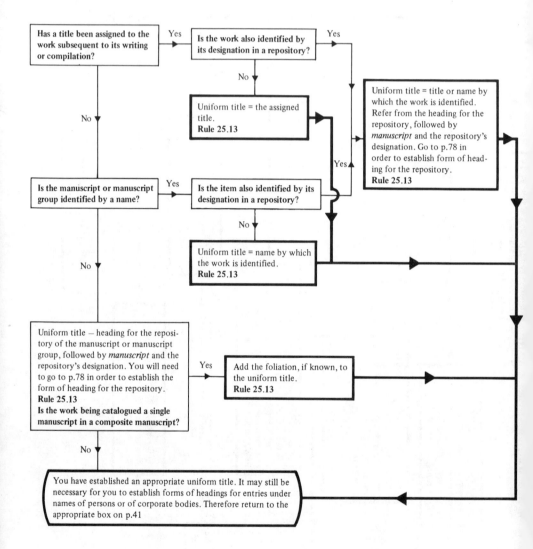

You have arrived here by deciding that:

An entry under TITLE is required, that a UNIFORM TITLE should be established and that the work does not fall into any of the special categories listed on p.44

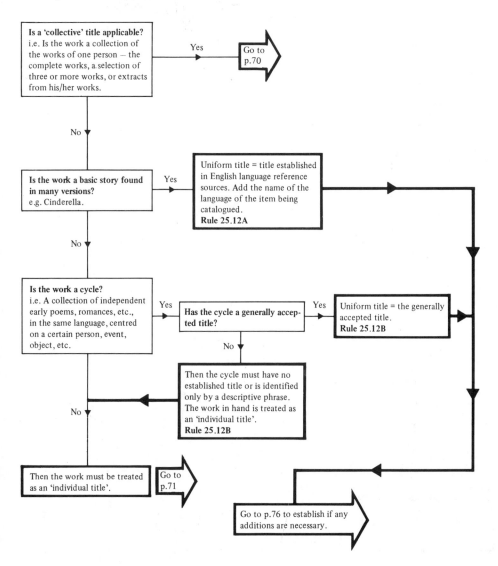

Is a 'collective' title applicable?
i.e. Is the work a collection of the works of one person – the complete works, a selection of three or more works, or extracts from his/her works.

Yes → Go to p.70

No ↓

Is the work a basic story found in many versions?
e.g. Cinderella.

Yes → Uniform title = title established in English language reference sources. Add the name of the language of the item being catalogued. **Rule 25.12A**

No ↓

Is the work a cycle?
i.e. A collection of independent early poems, romances, etc., in the same language, centred on a certain person, event, object, etc.

Yes → **Has the cycle a generally accepted title?**

Yes → Uniform title = the generally accepted title. **Rule 25.12B**

No ↓

Then the cycle must have no established title or is identified only by a descriptive phrase. The work in hand is treated as an 'individual title'. **Rule 25.12B**

No ↓

Then the work must be treated as an 'individual title'.

Go to p.71

Go to p.76 to establish if any additions are necessary.

70

You have arrived here by deciding that:
An entry under TITLE is required, that a UNIFORM TITLE should be established, the work does not fall into any of the categories listed on p.44 and that the work is a COLLECTIVE TITLE (as defined on p.69)

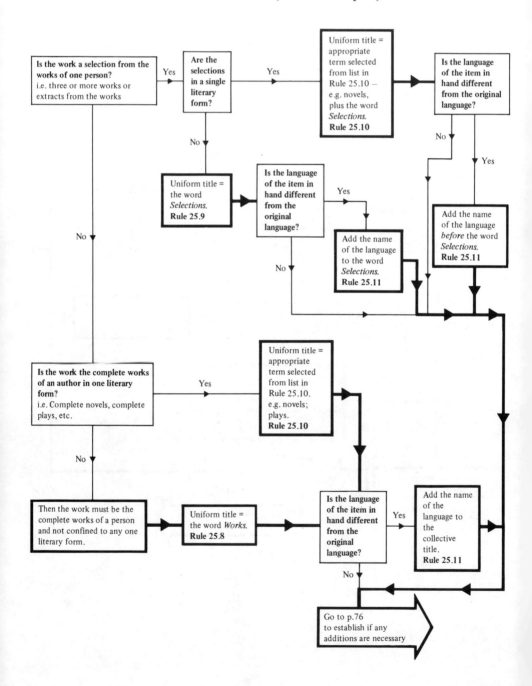

You have arrived here by deciding that:
An entry under TITLE is required, a UNIFORM TITLE should be established
lished, that the work does not fall into any of the special categories listed on
p.44 and that the work is an INDIVIDUAL TITLE.

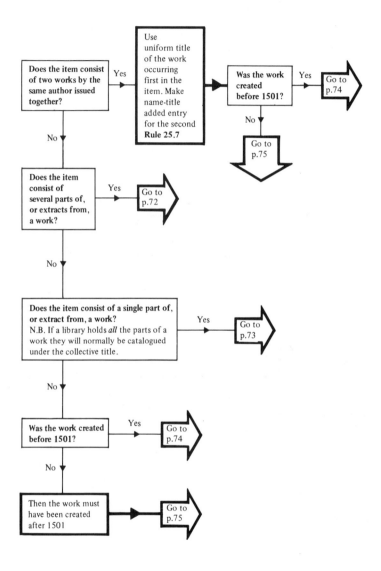

You have arrived here by deciding that:

An entry under TITLE is required, that a UNIFORM TITLE should be established, that the work does not fall into any of the special categories listed on p.44, that it is an INDIVIDUAL TITLE and that it consists of several PARTS of, or EXTRACTS from, a larger work.

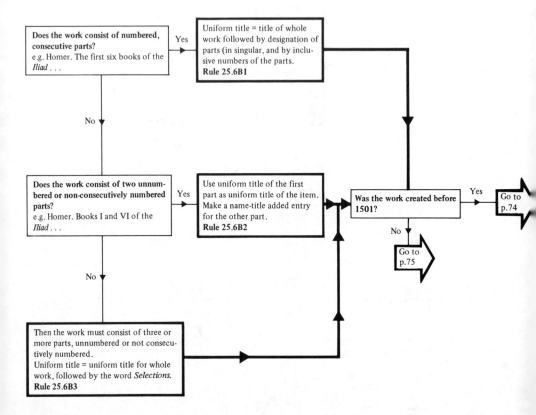

Does the work consist of numbered, consecutive parts?
e.g. Homer. The first six books of the *Iliad* . . .

Yes → Uniform title = title of whole work followed by designation of parts (in singular, and by inclusive numbers of the parts.
Rule 25.6B1

No ↓

Does the work consist of two unnumbered or non-consecutively numbered parts?
e.g. Homer. Books I and VI of the *Iliad* . . .

Yes → Use uniform title of the first part as uniform title of the item. Make a name-title added entry for the other part.
Rule 25.6B2

No ↓

Then the work must consist of three or more parts, unnumbered or not consecutively numbered.
Uniform title = uniform title for whole work, followed by the word *Selections*.
Rule 25.6B3

Was the work created before 1501?

Yes → Go to p.74

No ↓

Go to p.75

You have arrived here by deciding that:

An entry under TITLE is required, that a UNIFORM TITLE should be established, that the work does not fall into any of the special categories listed on p.44, that the item is an INDIVIDUAL TITLE and that it is a SINGLE PART of, or EXTRACT from, a work.

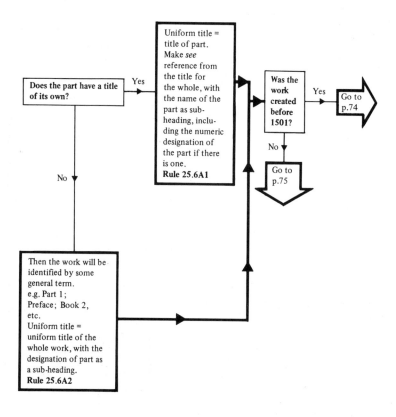

You have arrived here by deciding that:
An entry under TITLE is required, a UNIFORM TITLE should be established and that it is a single title for a work created before 1501.

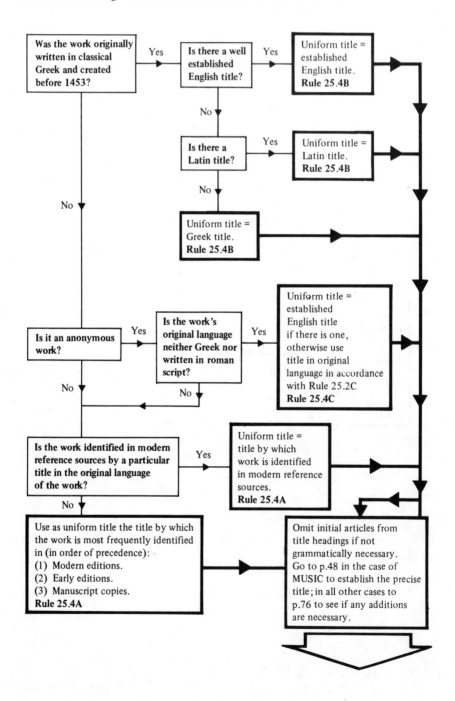

You have arrived here by deciding that:
An entry under TITLE is required, a UNIFORM TITLE should be established and that it is a SINGLE TITLE for a work created after 1500.

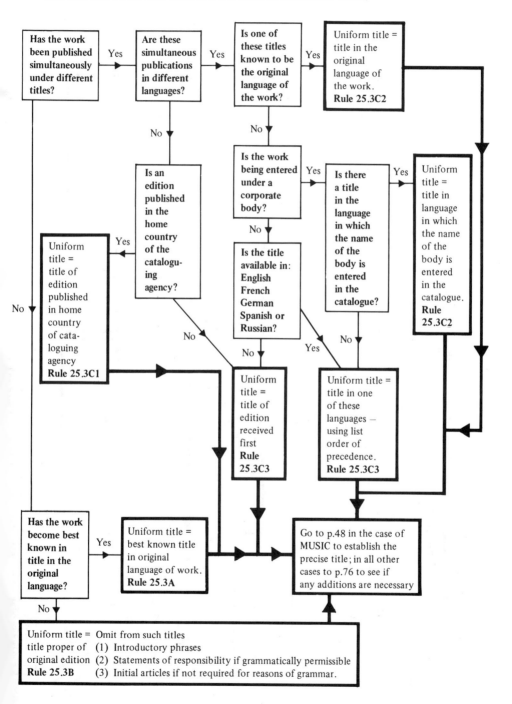

You have decided upon the UNIFORM TITLE.
Finally, it may be necessary to make some addition to this title in order to provide an absolute identification.

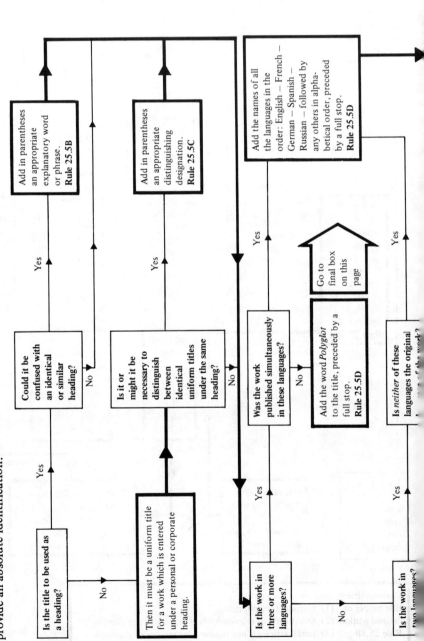

Is the title to be used as a heading?

Yes → Could it be confused with an identical or similar heading?

Yes → Add in parentheses an appropriate explanatory word or phrase. **Rule 25.5B**

No →

No → Then it must be a uniform title for a work which is entered under a personal or corporate heading.

Is it or might it be necessary to distinguish between identical uniform titles under the same heading?

Yes → Add in parentheses an appropriate distinguishing designation. **Rule 25.5C**

No →

Is the work in three or more languages?

Yes → Was the work published simultaneously in these languages?

Yes → Add the names of all the languages in the order: English — French — German — Spanish — Russian — followed by any others in alphabetical order, preceded by a full stop. **Rule 25.5D**

No → Add the word *Polyglot* to the title, preceded by a full stop. **Rule 25.5D**

Go to final box on this page

No → Is the work in two languages?

Yes → Is *neither* of these languages the original language of the work?

Yes →

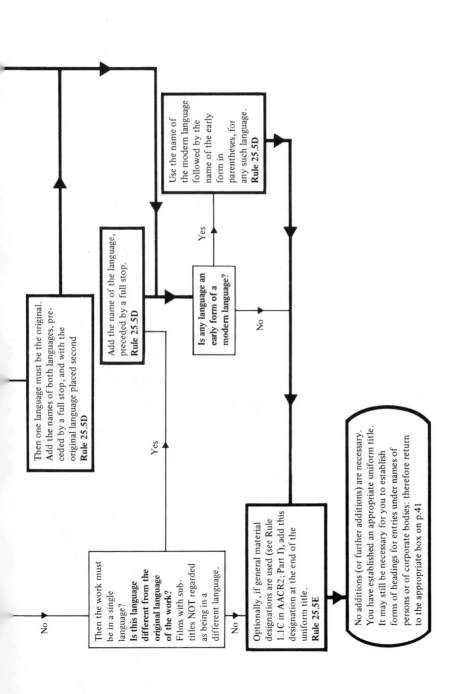

Then one language must be the original. Add the names of both languages, preceded by a full stop, and with the original language placed second **Rule 25.5D**

Add the name of the language, preceded by a full stop. **Rule 25.5D**

Use the name of the modern language followed by the name of the early form in parentheses, for any such language. **Rule 25.5D**

Is any language an early form of a modern language?

Yes

No

Then the work must be in a single language?

Is this language different from the original language of the work? Films with sub-titles NOT regarded as being in a different language.

Yes

No

No

Optionally, if general material designations are used (see Rule 1.1C in AACR2; Part I), add this designation at the end of the uniform title. **Rule 25.5E**

No additions (or further additions) are necessary. You have established an appropriate uniform title. It may still be necessary for you to establish forms of headings for entries under names of persons or of corporate bodies: therefore return to the appropriate box on p.41

You have arrived here by deciding that:
An entry under the name of a CORPORATE BODY is required.

Note

(1) **Romanization (Rule 24.1A)**
If the name of the body is in a language written in a non-roman script, romanize the name according to the transliteration table for that language adopted by the cataloguing agency. Refer from other romanizations as necessary.

(2) **Change of name (Rule 24.1B)**
If the name of a corporate body has changed (including change from one language to another) establish a new heading for works appearing under the new name, and connect the old and the new names by references.

e.g. Countryside Commission National Parks Commission
see also *see also*
National Parks Commission Countryside Commission
for earlier works of this body. for later works of this body.

(3) If the name of a corporate body consists of or contains initials, omit or include full stops and other marks of punctuation according to the predominant usage of the body. In case of doubt, omit the full stops, etc. Do not leave a space between a full stop, etc., and an initial following it. Do not leave spaces between the letters of an initialism written without full stops, etc. **(Rule 24.1)**

(4) **Omissions from corporate headings (Rule 24.5)**
   (a) Omit initial articles unless they are required for grammatical reasons. **(Rule 24.5A)**
   (b) Omit phrases citing honours awarded to the body. **(Rule 24.5B)**
   (c) Omit terms signifying the incorporation, ownership, status, etc. of organizations (e.g. Ltd., Pty., Inc.) unless they are an integral part of the name or are needed to make it clear that it is a corporate name. **(Rule 24.5C1-24.5C3)**
   Omit also abbreviations such as H.M.S. and U.S.S. occurring before the name of a ship. **(Rule 24.5C4)**

(5) **References**
Make references from other forms of name for a corporate body (i.e. those not adopted as entry headings) as instructed in **Rule 26.3**.

Certain categories of corporate bodies are treated in special ways. Therefore it is first of all necessary to establish if these special provisions apply.

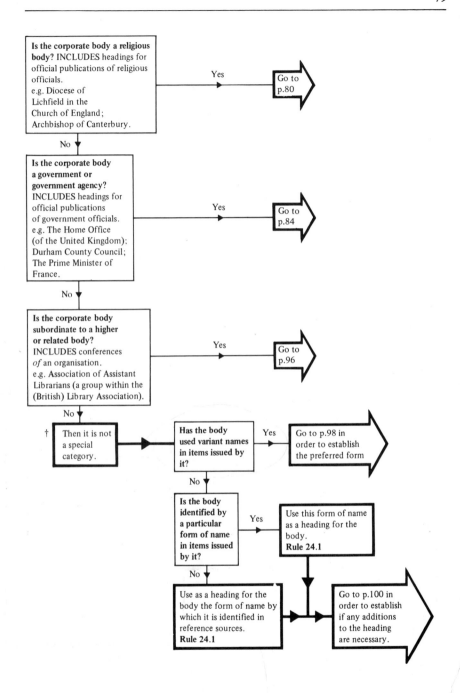

Is the corporate body a religious body? INCLUDES headings for official publications of religious officials.
e.g. Diocese of Lichfield in the Church of England; Archbishop of Canterbury.

Yes → Go to p.80

No ↓

Is the corporate body a government or government agency? INCLUDES headings for official publications of government officials.
e.g. The Home Office (of the United Kingdom); Durham County Council; The Prime Minister of France.

Yes → Go to p.84

No ↓

Is the corporate body subordinate to a higher or related body? INCLUDES conferences *of* an organisation.
e.g. Association of Assistant Librarians (a group within the (British) Library Association).

Yes → Go to p.96

No ↓

† Then it is not a special category.

→ **Has the body used variant names in items issued by it?**

Yes → Go to p.98 in order to establish the preferred form

No ↓

Is the body identified by a particular form of name in items issued by it?

Yes → Use this form of name as a heading for the body. **Rule 24.1**

No ↓

Use as a heading for the body the form of name by which it is identified in reference sources. **Rule 24.1**

→ Go to p.100 in order to establish if any additions to the heading are necessary.

You have arrived here by deciding that:
An entry under the name of a CORPORATE BODY is required and that you are dealing with a RELIGIOUS BODY.

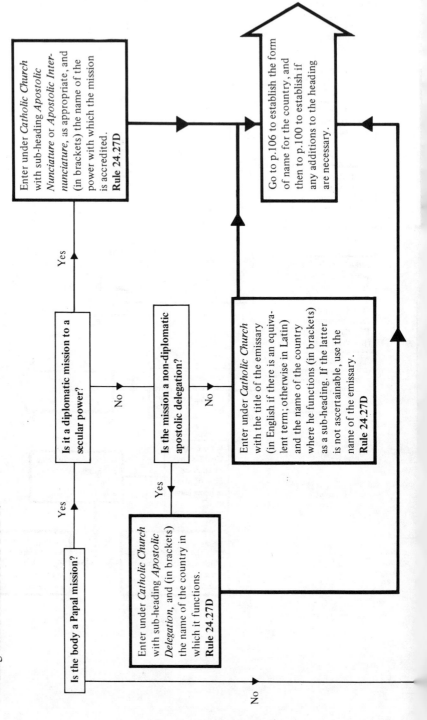

Is the body a Papal mission?

Yes → **Is it a diplomatic mission to a secular power?**

Yes → Enter under *Catholic Church* with sub-heading *Apostolic Nunciature* or *Apostolic Inter-nunciature*, as appropriate, and (in brackets) the name of the power with which the mission is accredited. **Rule 24.27D**

No → **Is the mission a non-diplomatic apostolic delegation?**

Yes → Enter under *Catholic Church* with sub-heading *Apostolic Delegation*, and (in brackets) the name of the country in which it functions. **Rule 24.27D**

No → Enter under *Catholic Church* with the title of the emissary (in English if there is an equivalent term; otherwise in Latin) and the name of the country where he functions (in brackets) as a sub-heading. If the latter is not ascertainable, use the name of the emissary. **Rule 24.27D**

Go to p.106 to establish the form of name for the country, and then to p.100 to establish if any additions to the heading are necessary.

No

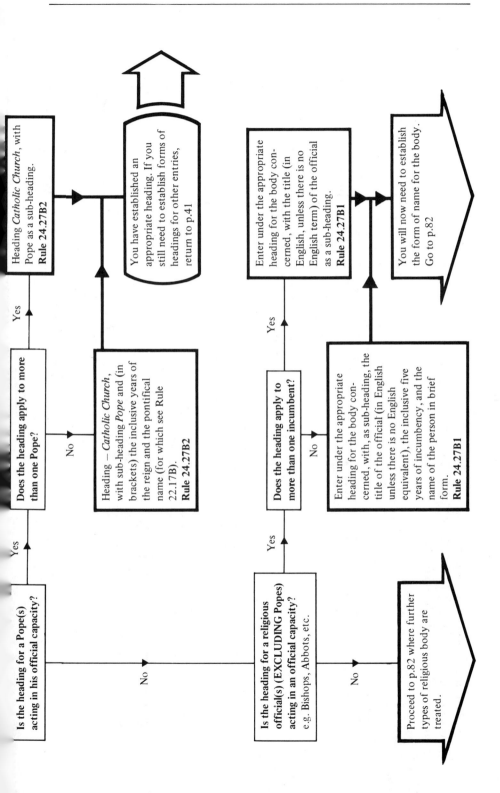

Is the heading for a Pope(s) acting in his official capacity?

Yes →

Does the heading apply to more than one Pope?

Yes → Heading *Catholic Church*, with Pope as a sub-heading. **Rule 24.27B2**

No → Heading – *Catholic Church*, with sub-heading *Pope* and (in brackets) the inclusive years of the reign and the pontifical name (for which see Rule 22.17B). **Rule 24.27B2**

You have established an appropriate heading. If you still need to establish forms of headings for other entries, return to p.41

No ↓

Is the heading for a religious official(s) (EXCLUDING Popes) acting in an official capacity? e.g. Bishops, Abbots, etc.

Yes →

Does the heading apply to more than one incumbent?

Yes → Enter under the appropriate heading for the body concerned, with the title (in English, unless there is no English term) of the official as a sub-heading. **Rule 24.27B1**

No → Enter under the appropriate heading for the body concerned, with, as sub-heading, the title of the official (in English unless there is no English equivalent), the inclusive five years of incumbency, and the name of the person in brief form. **Rule 24.27B1**

You will now need to establish the form of name for the body. Go to p.82

No ↓

Proceed to p.82 where further types of religious body are treated.

You have arrived here by deciding that:
An entry under the name of a **CORPORATE BODY** is required and that you are dealing with a **RELIGIOUS BODY**.

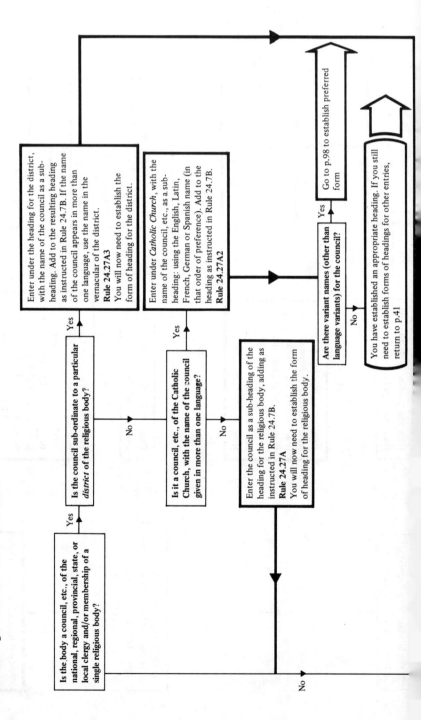

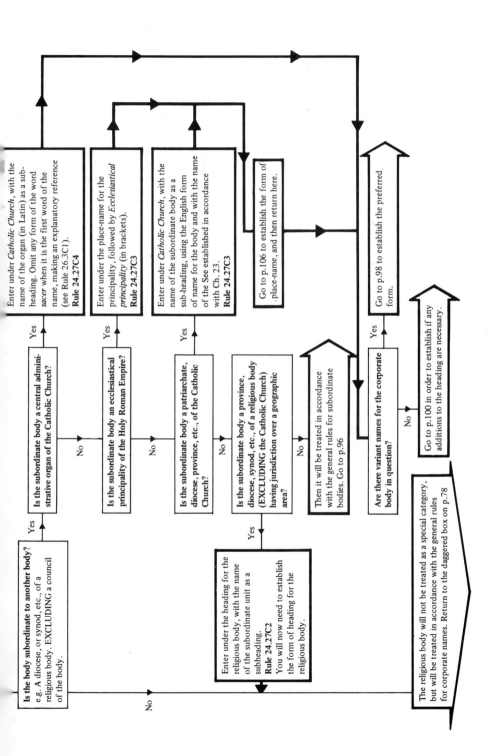

You have arrived here by deciding that:

An entry under the name of a CORPORATE BODY is required and that the corporate body is a GOVERNMENT or a GOVERNMENT AGENCY, or you are dealing with the heading for a GOVERNMENT OFFICIAL writing in his official capacity.

Note

Some government bodies or agencies are entered directly under their names, others are entered as sub-headings of the name of the appropriate government. The algorithms which follow will indicate which solution applies in a particular instance.

When you are directed to 'enter under the name of a government', use the 'conventional name' of the government. i.e. The geographic name, established in accordance with chapter 23 of AACR2 (which is analyzed on p.106 of this text. In exceptional cases, when the official name of the government is in common use, this is preferred. e.g. Greater London Council *not* London (England).

Some government bodies require special treatment. Choose from the types listed opposite.

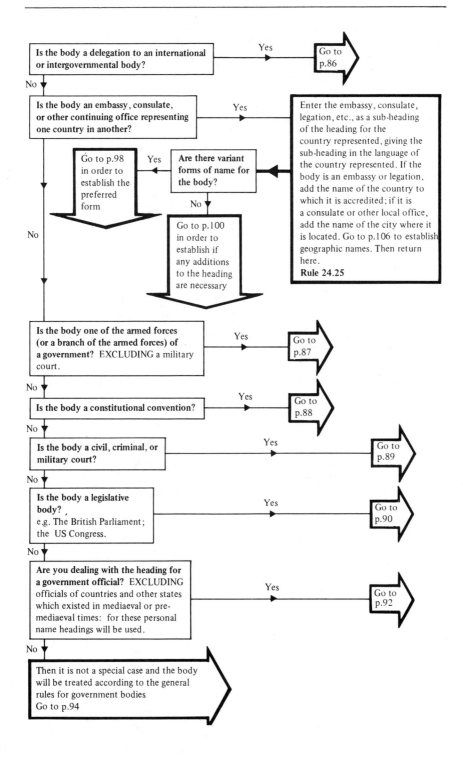

Is the body a delegation to an international or intergovernmental body? — Yes → Go to p.86

No ↓

Is the body an embassy, consulate, or other continuing office representing one country in another? — Yes → Enter the embassy, consulate, legation, etc., as a sub-heading of the heading for the country represented, giving the sub-heading in the language of the country represented. If the body is an embassy or legation, add the name of the country to which it is accredited; if it is a consulate or other local office, add the name of the city where it is located. Go to p.106 to establish geographic names. Then return here.
Rule 24.25

Go to p.98 in order to establish the preferred form ← Yes — Are there variant forms of name for the body? ←

No ↓

Go to p.100 in order to establish if any additions to the heading are necessary

No ↓

Is the body one of the armed forces (or a branch of the armed forces) of a government? EXCLUDING a military court. — Yes → Go to p.87

No ↓

Is the body a constitutional convention? — Yes → Go to p.88

No ↓

Is the body a civil, criminal, or military court? — Yes → Go to p.89

No ↓

Is the body a legislative body? , e.g. The British Parliament; the US Congress. — Yes → Go to p.90

No ↓

Are you dealing with the heading for a government official? EXCLUDING officials of countries and other states which existed in mediaeval or pre-mediaeval times: for these personal name headings will be used. — Yes → Go to p.92

No ↓

Then it is not a special case and the body will be treated according to the general rules for government bodies
Go to p.94

You have arrived here by deciding that:
An entry under the name of a CORPORATE BODY is required, the body is a GOVERNMENT AGENCY and that it is a DELEGATION TO AN INTERNATIONAL or INTERGOVERNMENTAL BODY.

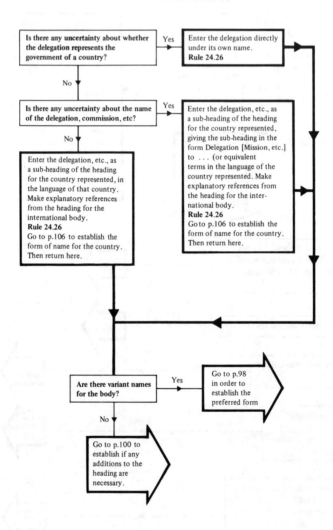

You have arrived here by deciding that:
An entry under the name of a CORPORATE BODY is required, the body is a GOVERNMENT AGENCY and that it is one of the ARMED FORCES of a government.

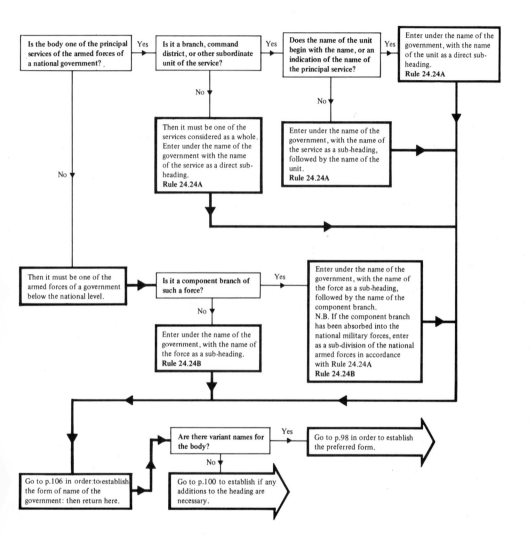

88

You have arrived here by deciding that:
An entry under the name of a CORPORATE BODY is required, the body is a
GOVERNMENT AGENCY and that it is a CONSTITUTIONAL CONVENTION.

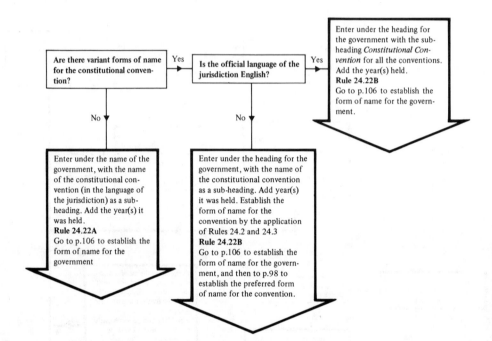

You have arrived here by deciding that:
An entry under the name of a CORPORATE BODY is required, the body is a
CORPORATE BODY and that it is a COURT OF LAW.

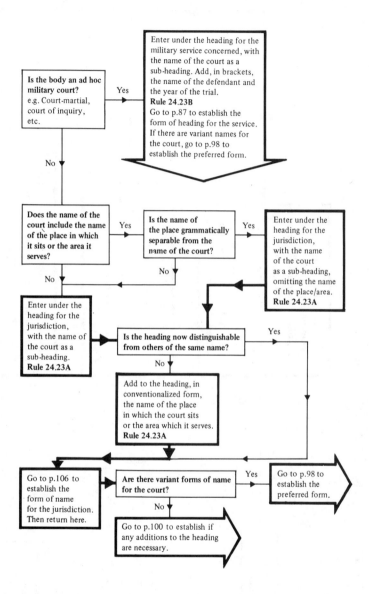

You have arrived here by deciding that:
An entry under the name of a CORPORATE BODY is required, the body is a GOVERNMENT AGENCY, and it is a LEGISLATIVE BODY.

Is the body a *chamber* of a particular legislature?

— No →

Is the body a legislative committee of the U.S. Congress?

— No →

Is the body a committee or other subordinate unit of a legislature or chamber of a legislature? (EXCLUDING legislative sub-committees of the U.S. Congress).

Yes →

Enter under the heading for the government, with a sub-heading consisting of the name of the legislature, followed by the name of the chamber.
Rule 24.21A
Go to p.106 to establish the form of name for the government. Then return here.

Yes →

Enter under United States. *Congress*, with a sub-heading consisting of the name of the chamber (if appropriate), the name of the parent committee, and the name of the sub-committee.
Rule 24.21C

Yes →

Enter under the heading for the government, with a sub-heading consisting of the name of the legislature, the name of the chamber (if appropriate), and the name of the committee or subordinate unit.
Rule 24.21B
Go to p.106 to establish the form of name for the government. Then return here.

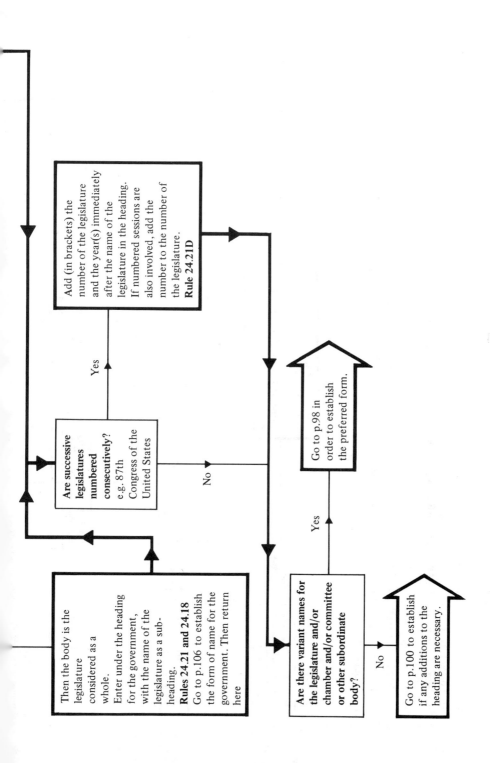

Then the body is the legislature considered as a whole.
Enter under the heading for the government, with the name of the legislature as a sub-heading.
Rules 24.21 and 24.18
Go to p.106 to establish the form of name for the government. Then return here

Are successive legislatures numbered consecutively?
e.g. 87th Congress of the United States

Yes

Add (in brackets) the number of the legislature and the year(s) immediately after the name of the legislature in the heading. If numbered sessions are also involved, add the number to the number of the legislature. **Rule 24.21D**

No

Go to p.98 in order to establish the preferred form.

Are there variant names for the legislature and/or chamber and/or committee or other subordinate body?

Yes

No

Go to p.100 to establish if any additions to the heading are necessary.

You have arrived here by deciding that:
An entry under the name of a CORPORATE BODY is required and that the heading is for a GOVERNMENT OFFICIAL acting in his/her official capacity.

Note
If a heading is established for the official as a person in addition to the heading for his/her official title, make an explanatory reference under the heading for the official title. See Rule 26.3C1.

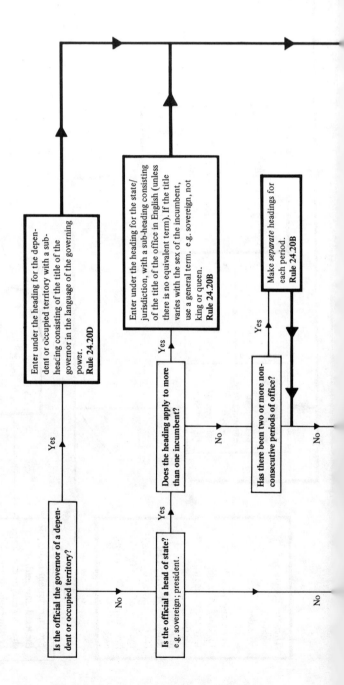

Is the official the governor of a dependent or occupied territory?

No → Yes

Enter under the heading for the dependent or occupied territory with a sub-heading consisting of the title of the governor in the language of the governing power.
Rule 24.20D

Is the official a head of state? e.g. sovereign; president.

Yes → Does the heading apply to more than one incumbent?

Yes → Enter under the heading for the state/jurisdiction, with a sub-heading consisting of the title of the office in English (unless there is no equivalent term). If title varies with the sex of the incumbent, use a general term. e.g. sovereign, not king or queen.
Rule 24.20B

No →

Has there been two or more non-consecutive periods of office?

Yes → Make *separate* headings for each period.
Rule 24.20B

No →

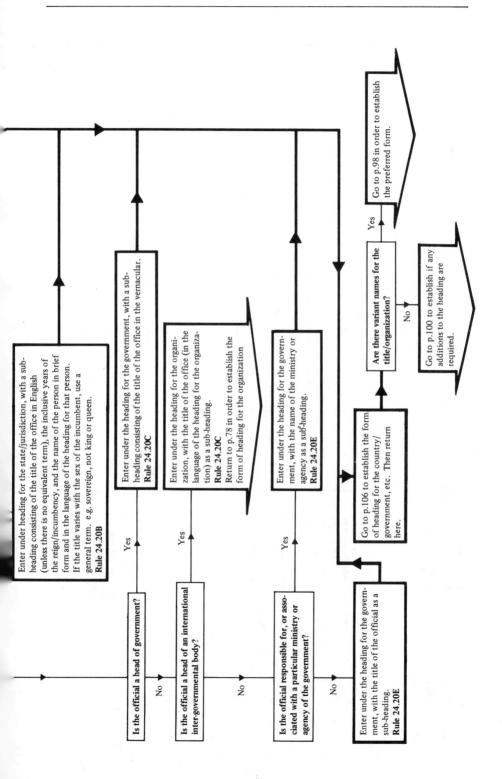

You have arrived here by deciding that:
An entry under the name of a CORPORATE BODY is required, the body is a GOVERNMENT AGENCY and that it is NOT one of the 'special cases' identified on p.84

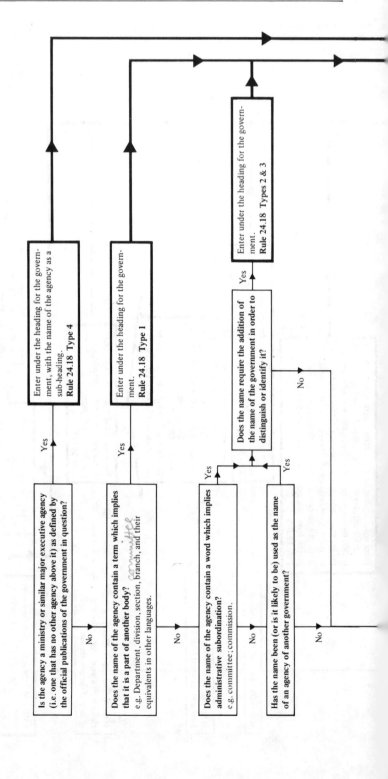

Is the agency a ministry or similar major executive agency (i.e. one that has no other agency above it) as defined by the official publications of the government in question?

— Yes → Enter under the heading for the government, with the name of the agency as a sub-heading.
Rule 24.18 Type 4

No

Does the name of the agency contain a term which implies that it is a part of another body?
e.g. Department, division, section, branch, and their equivalents in other languages.

— Yes → Enter under the heading for the government.
Rule 24.18 Type 1

No

Does the name of the agency contain a word which implies administrative subordination?
e.g. committee; commission.

Yes

No

Has the name been (or is it likely to be) used as the name of an agency of another government?

Yes

No

Does the name require the addition of the name of the government in order to distinguish or identify it?

— Yes → Enter under the heading for the government.
Rule 24.18 Types 2 & 3

No

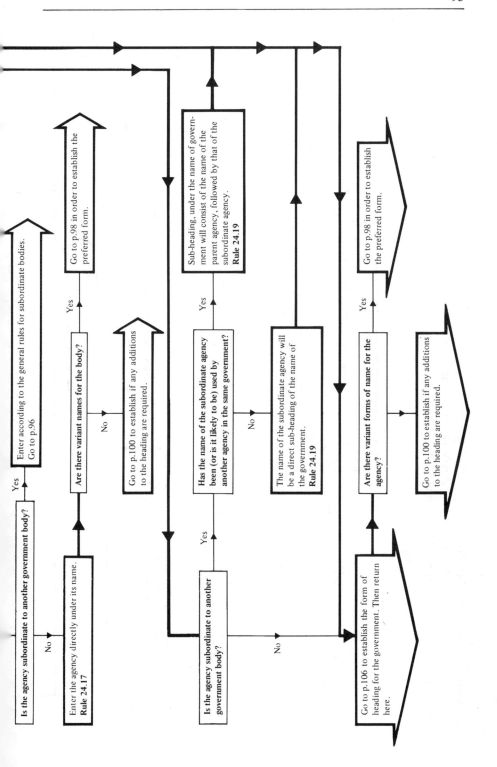

Is the agency subordinate to another government body?

Yes — Enter according to the general rules for subordinate bodies. Go to p.96

No — Enter the agency directly under its name. Rule 24.17

Are there variant names for the body?

Yes — Go to p.98 in order to establish the preferred form.

No — Go to p.100 to establish if any additions to the heading are required.

Is the agency subordinate to another government body?

Has the name of the subordinate agency been (or is it likely to be) used by another agency in the same government?

Yes — Sub-heading, under the name of government will consist of the name of the parent agency, followed by that of the subordinate agency. Rule 24.19

No — The name of the subordinate agency will be a direct sub-heading of the name of the government. Rule 24.19

Are there variant forms of name for the agency?

Yes — Go to p.98 in order to establish the preferred form.

Go to p.100 to establish if any additions to the heading are required.

Go to p.106 to establish the form of heading for the government. Then return here.

You have arrived here by deciding that:
An entry under the name of a CORPORATE BODY is required and that the body is SUBORDINATE or RELATED to another body.

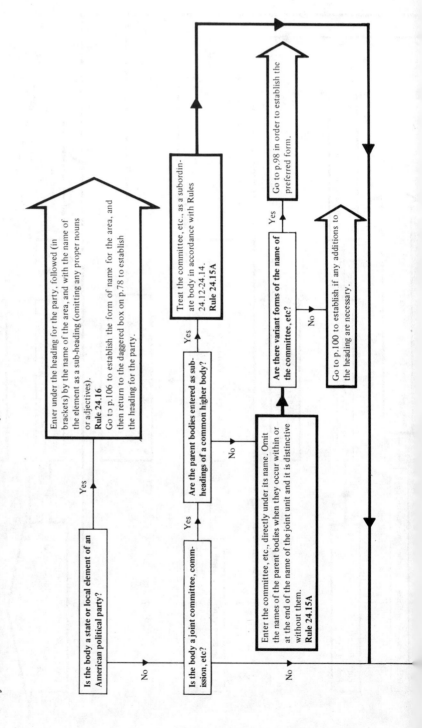

Is the body a state or local element of an American political party?

No

Yes → Enter under the heading for the party, followed (in brackets) by the name of the area, and with the name of the element as a sub-heading (omitting any proper nouns or adjectives). **Rule 24.16**

Go to p.106 to establish the form of name for the area, and then return to the daggered box on p.78 to establish the heading for the party.

Is the body a joint committee, commission, etc?

No

Yes → **Are the parent bodies entered as sub-headings of a common higher body?**

Yes → Treat the committee, etc., as a subordinate body in accordance with Rules 24.12-24.14. **Rule 24.15A**

No

Enter the committee, etc., directly under its name. Omit the names of the parent bodies when they occur within or at the end of the name of the joint unit and it is distinctive without them. **Rule 24.15A**

Are there variant forms of the name of the committee, etc?

Yes → Go to p.98 in order to establish the preferred form.

No → Go to p.100 to establish if any additions to the heading are necessary.

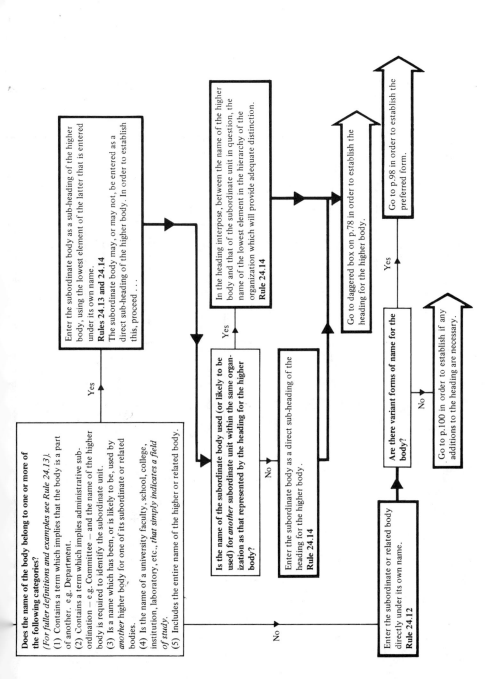

Does the name of the body belong to one or more of the following categories?

[For fuller definitions and examples see Rule 24.13].

(1) Contains a term which implies that the body is a part of another. e.g. Department.

(2) Contains a term which implies administrative sub-ordination — e.g. Committee — and the name of the higher body is required to identify the subordinate unit.

(3) Is a name which has been, or is likely to be, used by *another* higher body for one of its subordinate or related bodies.

(4) Is the name of a university faculty, school, college, institution, laboratory, etc., *that simply indicates a field of study*.

(5) Includes the entire name of the higher or related body.

Yes →

Enter the subordinate body as a sub-heading of the higher body, using the lowest element of the latter that is entered under its own name.
Rules 24.13 and 24.14
The subordinate body may, or may not, be entered as a direct sub-heading of the higher body. In order to establish this, proceed . . . .

Is the name of the subordinate body used (or likely to be used) for *another* subordinate unit within the same organization as that represented by the heading for the higher body?

Yes →

In the heading interpose, between the name of the higher body and that of the subordinate unit in question, the name of the lowest element in the hierarchy of the organization which will provide adequate distinction.
Rule 24.14

No →

Enter the subordinate body as a direct sub-heading of the heading for the higher body.
Rule 24.14

Go to daggered box on p.78 in order to establish the heading for the higher body.

Go to p.98 in order to establish the preferred form.

No →

Enter the subordinate or related body directly under its own name.
Rule 24.12

Are there variant forms of name for the body?

Yes → Go to daggered box on p.78 in order to establish the heading for the higher body.

No → Go to p.100 in order to establish if any additions to the heading are necessary.

You have arrived here by deciding that:
An entry under the name of a CORPORATE BODY is required and that there are VARIANT FORMS of the body's name.

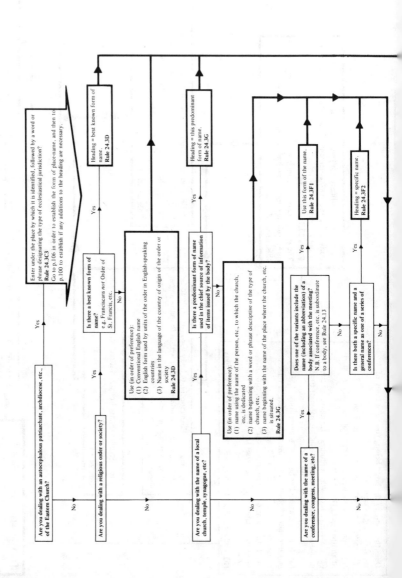

Are you dealing with an autocephalous patriarchate, archdiocese, etc., of the Eastern Church?

Yes → Enter under the place by which it is identified, followed by a word or phrase designating the type of ecclesiastical jurisdiction? **Rule 24.3C3**
Go to p.106 in order to establish the form of place-name, and then to p.100 to establish if any additions to the heading are necessary.

No ↓

Are you dealing with a religious order or society?

Yes → **Is there a best known form of name?** e.g. Franciscans *not* Order of St. Francis, etc.

 Yes → Heading = best known form of name. **Rule 24.3D**

 No → Use (in order of preference): (1) Conventional English name (2) English form used by units of the order in English-speaking countries (3) Name in the language of the country of origin of the order or society **Rule 24.3D**

No ↓

Are you dealing with the name of a local church, temple, synagogue, etc.?

Yes → **Is there a predominant form of name used in the chief source of information of items issued by the body?**

 Yes → Heading = this predominant form of name. **Rule 24.3G**

 No → Use (in order of preference): (1) name using the name of the person, etc., to which the church, etc. is dedicated (2) name beginning with a word or phrase descriptive of the type of church, etc. (3) name beginning with the name of the place where the church, etc. is situated. **Rule 24.3G**

No ↓

Are you dealing with the name of a conference, congress, meeting, etc.?

Yes → **Does one of the variants include the name (including an abbreviation) of a body associated with the meeting?** N.B. If conference, etc. is subordinate to a body, see Rule 24.13

 Yes → Use this form of the name. **Rule 24.3F1**

 No → **Is there both a specific name and a general name as one of a series of conferences?**

 Yes → Heading = specific name. **Rule 24.3F2**

 No ↓

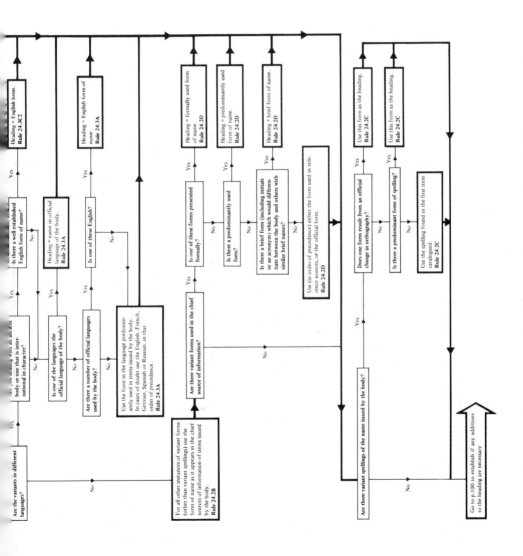

You have arrived here by deciding that:
An entry under the name of a CORPORATE BODY is required. You have determined the basis of the form of heading for the body. Finally, you must establish if any further ADDITIONS to the heading are necessary.

Note

(1) All additions specified below are given in parentheses.
(2) Where the addition of a geographic name is required its form is established by the application of chapter 23 of the Rules: treated on p.106 of the algorithm.

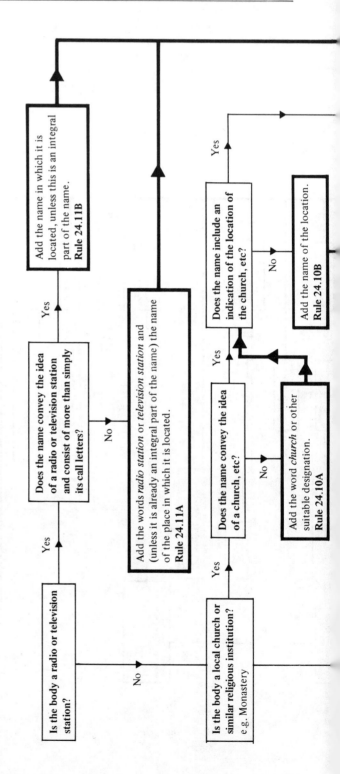

Is the body a radio or television station?

Does the name convey the idea of a radio or television station and consist of more than simply its call letters?

Yes → Add the name in which it is located, unless this is an integral part of the name. **Rule 24.11B**

No → Add the words *radio station* or *television station* and (unless it is already an integral part of the name) the name of the place in which it is located. **Rule 24.11A**

Is the body a local church or similar religious institution? e.g. Monastery

Does the name convey the idea of a church, etc?

Yes → Does the name include an indication of the location of the church, etc?

Yes

No → Add the name of the location. **Rule 24.10B**

No → Add the word *church* or other suitable designation. **Rule 24.10A**

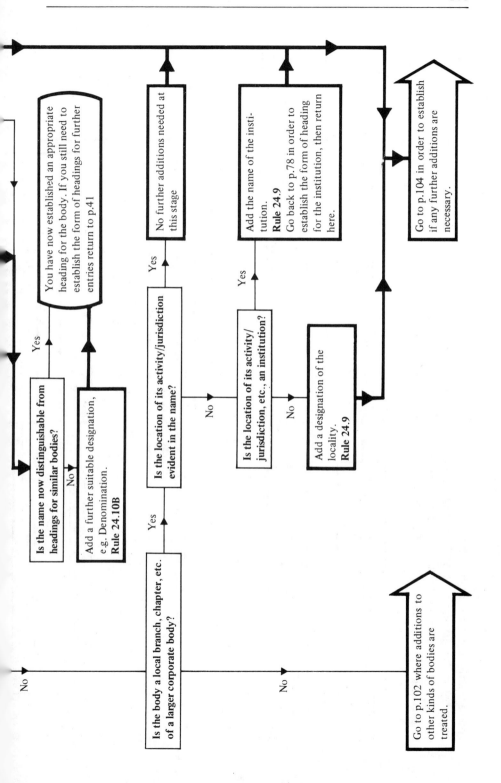

You have arrived here by deciding that:
An entry under the name of a CORPORATE BODY is required. You have determined the basis of the form of heading for the body and are now in process of checking to see if any further ADDITIONS to the heading are necessary.

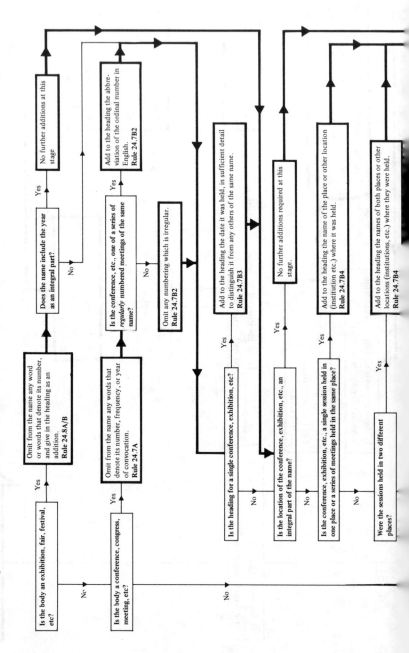

Is the body an exhibition, fair, festival, etc? — Yes → Omit from the name any word or words that denote its number, and give in the heading as an addition. **Rule 24.8A/B** → Does the name include the year as an integral part? — Yes → No further additions at this stage; No →

Is the body a conference, congress, meeting, etc? — Yes → Omit from the name any words that denote its number, frequency, or year of convocation. **Rule 24.7A** → Is the conference, etc., one of a series of *regularly* numbered meetings of the same name? — Yes → Add to the heading the abbreviation of the ordinal number in English. **Rule 24.7B2**; No → Omit any numbering which is irregular. **Rule 24.7B2**

Is the heading for a single conference, exhibition, etc? — Yes → Add to the heading the date it was held, in sufficient detail to distinguish it from any others of the same name. **Rule 24.7B3**; No →

Is the location of the conference, exhibition, etc., an integral part of the name? — Yes → No further additions required at this stage; No →

Is the conference, exhibition, etc., a single session held in one place or a series of meetings held in the same place? — Yes → Add to the heading the name of the place or other location (institution etc.) where it was held. **Rule 24.7B4**; No →

Were the sessions held in two different places? — Yes → Add to the heading the names of both places or other locations (institutions, etc.) where they were held. **Rule 24.7B4**

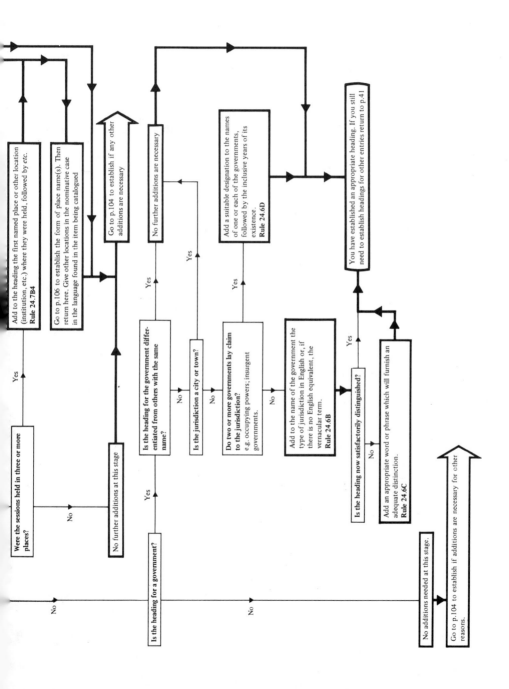

Were the sessions held in three or more places?

Yes → Add to the heading the first named place or other location (institution, etc.) where they were held, followed by *etc.* **Rule 24.7B4**

Go to p.106 to establish the form of place name(s). Then return here. Give other locations in the nominative case in the language found in the item being catalogued

No further additions at this stage

Go to p.104 to establish if any other additions are necessary

Is the heading for a government?

No

Is the heading for the government differentiated from others with the same name?

Yes → No further additions are necessary

No → Is the jurisdiction a city or town?

Yes

No → Do two or more governments lay claim to the jurisdiction? e.g. occupying powers; insurgent governments.

Yes → Add a suitable designation to the names of one or each of the governments, followed by the inclusive years of its existence. **Rule 24.6D**

No → Add to the name of the government the type of jurisdiction in English or, if there is no English equivalent, the vernacular term. **Rule 24.6B**

Is the heading now satisfactorily distinguished?

Yes

No → Add an appropriate word or phrase which will furnish an adequate distinction. **Rule 24.6C**

You have established an appropriate heading. If you still need to establish headings for other entries return to p.41

No additions needed at this stage.

Go to p.104 to establish if additions are necessary for other reasons.

You have arrived here by deciding that:

An entry under the name of a CORPORATE BODY is required. You have determined the basis of a form of heading for the body and are now in process of checking to see if any further ADDITIONS to the heading are necessary.

Note

If the name of a local jurisdiction or geographic locality is used as an addition to the name of a body, and the name of the locality, etc. has changed during the lifetime of the body, use the latest name for the locality, etc. that has been used in the lifetime of the body. **Rule 24.4C6**

Remember

All additions specified below are given in parentheses, *and* geographic names are established in accordance with chapter 23 of the Rules: treated on p.106 of the algorithm.

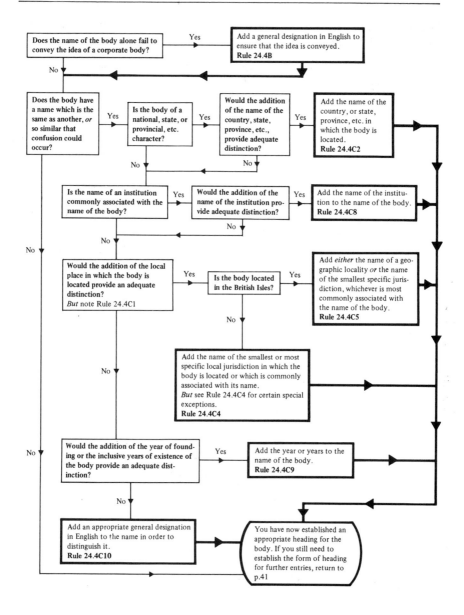

You have arrived here by deciding that you need to establish the form of a GEOGRAPHIC NAME to use:

      (a) to distinguish between corporate bodies of the same name

or (b) as an addition to other corporate names,

or (c) as a heading for a government.

Note

(1) *Changes of name.* If the name of a place changes (whether the name of a government or the name of a place being added to a heading) use the name appropriate in time for the heading under consideration. **See Rule 23.3.** This decision having been made, the *form* of the name will then be determined by using the algorithm which follows.

(2) *Form of name for the United Kingdom.* The rules in chapter 23, and examples elsewhere in AACR2, imply the use of the form 'United Kingdom' for the geo-political entity of the 'United Kingdom of Great Britain and Northern Ireland'. However, the form traditionally used in catalogues, etc., for this jurisdiction is 'Great Britain'. Both the British Library and the Library of Congress have indicated their intentions to retain 'Great Britain' in their cataloguing procedures — and the solutions to the examples accompanying this text conform to this decision. i.e. they use the form 'Great Britain'.

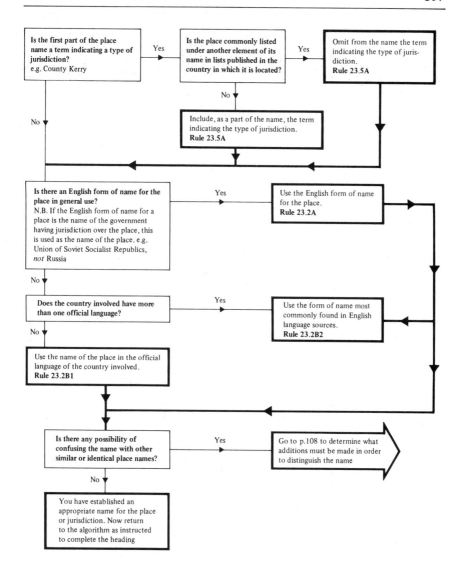

Is the first part of the place name a term indicating a type of jurisdiction?
e.g. County Kerry

Yes →

Is the place commonly listed under another element of its name in lists published in the country in which it is located?

Yes →

Omit from the name the term indicating the type of jurisdiction.
Rule 23.5A

No ↓

Include, as a part of the name, the term indicating the type of jurisdiction.
Rule 23.5A

No ↓

Is there an English form of name for the place in general use?
N.B. If the English form of name for a place is the name of the government having jurisdiction over the place, this is used as the name of the place. e.g. Union of Soviet Socialist Republics, *not* Russia

Yes →

Use the English form of name for the place.
Rule 23.2A

No ↓

Does the country involved have more than one official language?

Yes →

Use the form of name most commonly found in English language sources.
Rule 23.2B2

No ↓

Use the name of the place in the official language of the country involved.
Rule 23.2B1

Is there any possibility of confusing the name with other similar or identical place names?

Yes →

Go to p.108 to determine what additions must be made in order to distinguish the name

No ↓

You have established an appropriate name for the place or jurisdiction. Now return to the algorithm as instructed to complete the heading

You have arrived here by deciding that you need to make some ADDITIONS to a GEOGRAPHICAL NAME in order to distinguish between identical or similar names for places or jurisdictions.

Note

(1) All additions to place names as entry elements are given in parentheses. e.g. Budapest (Hungary).

(2) If the place name is being used as an addition, precede the name of the larger place by a comma. e.g. St. Peter's Church (York,England). **Rule 23.4A.**

(3) Place names used as additions may be abbreviated in accordance with the instructions in Appendix B.14 of the Rules. **Rule 23.4B.**

(4) Note certain options concerning additions detailed in Rule 23.4B.

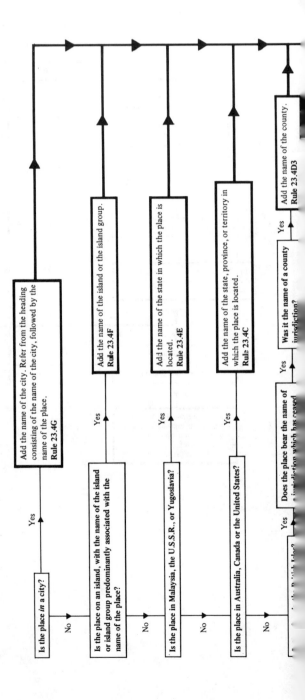

Is the place *in* a city? — Yes → Add the name of the city. Refer from the heading consisting of the name of the city, followed by the name of the place. **Rule 23.4G**

Is the place on an island, with the name of the island or island group predominantly associated with the name of the place? — Yes → Add the name of the island or the island group. **Rule 23.4F**

Is the place in Malaysia, the U.S.S.R., or Yugoslavia? — Yes → Add the name of the state in which the place is located. **Rule 23.4E**

Is the place in Australia, Canada or the United States? — Yes → Add the name of the state, province, or territory in which the place is located. **Rule 23.4C**

Does the place bear the name of a jurisdiction which has ceased — Yes → Was it the name of a county jurisdiction? — Yes → Add the name of the county. **Rule 23.4D3**

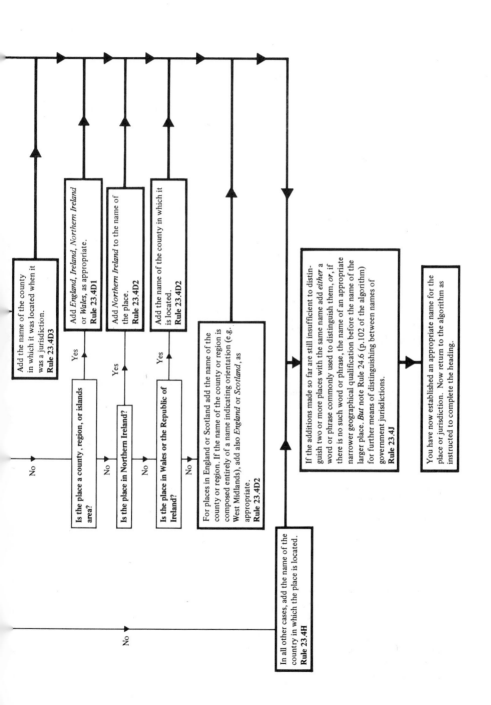

Add the name of the county in which it was located when it was a jurisdiction. **Rule 23.4D3**

Is the place a county, region, or islands area?
— Yes → Add *England*, *Ireland*, *Northern Ireland* or *Wales*, as appropriate. **Rule 23.4D1**
— No

Is the place in Northern Ireland?
— Yes → Add *Northern Ireland* to the name of the place. **Rule 23.4D2**
— No

Is the place in Wales or the Republic of Ireland?
— Yes → Add the name of the county in which it is located. **Rule 23.4D2**
— No

For places in England or Scotland add the name of the county or region. If the name of the county or region is composed entirely of a name indicating orientation (e.g. West Midlands), add also *England* or *Scotland*, as appropriate. **Rule 23.4D2**

In all other cases, add the name of the country in which the place is located. **Rule 23.4H**

If the additions made so far are still insufficient to distinguish two or more places with the same name add *either* a word or phrase commonly used to distinguish them, *or*, if there is no such word or phrase, the name of an appropriate narrower geographical qualification before the name of the larger place. *But* note Rule 24.6 (p.102 of the algorithm) for further means of distinguishing between names of government jurisdictions. **Rule 23.4J**

You have now established an appropriate name for the place or jurisdiction. Now return to the algorithm as instructed to complete the heading.

You have arrived here by deciding that:
An entry under the name of a PERSON is required.

Note

(1) The basis of the heading for a person is the name by which he or she is commonly identified. This may be the person's real name, pseudonym, title of nobility, initials, nickname or other appellation. **Rule 21.1A.**

(2) Establish the name by which a person is commonly identified from the *chief source of information* (see Rule 1.0A in Part I of the Rules) of the works of that person issued in his or her language. If the person works in a non-verbal context (e.g. a painter, a sculptor) or is not known primarily as an author, determine the name by which he or she is commonly known from reference sources issued in his or her language or country of residence or activity. **Rule 22.1B**

(3) Accents and other diacritical marks are included in the name, and are supplied if they are an integral part of the name but have been omitted in the source from which the name is taken. **Rule 22.1D1.**

(4) Hyphens are retained in the name if they are used by the bearer of the name or if they are prescribed by the romanization system adapted by the cataloguing agency. However, hyphens which join a person's fore-name(s) to the surname are omitted. **Rule 22.1D2.**

A person may be known by *different names* (e.g. the real name and a pseud-onym), or by *different forms of the same name* (e.g. Joan of Arc *and* Jeanne d'Arc). If so, you must first decide which of the names (or different forms of the name) you should prefer as the heading for that person.

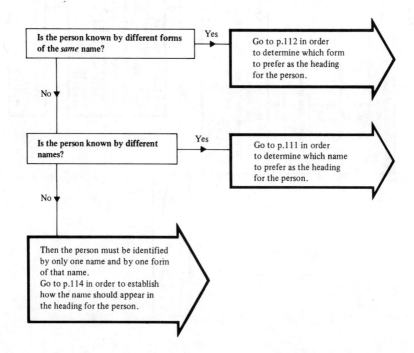

Is the person known by different forms of the *same* name? — Yes → Go to p.112 in order to determine which form to prefer as the heading for the person.

No ↓

Is the person known by different names? — Yes → Go to p.111 in order to determine which name to prefer as the heading for the person.

No ↓

Then the person must be identified by only one name and by one form of that name.
Go to p.114 in order to establish how the name should appear in the heading for the person.

You have arrived here by deciding that:

An entry under the name of a PERSON is required and that the person is or has been known by DIFFERENT NAMES.

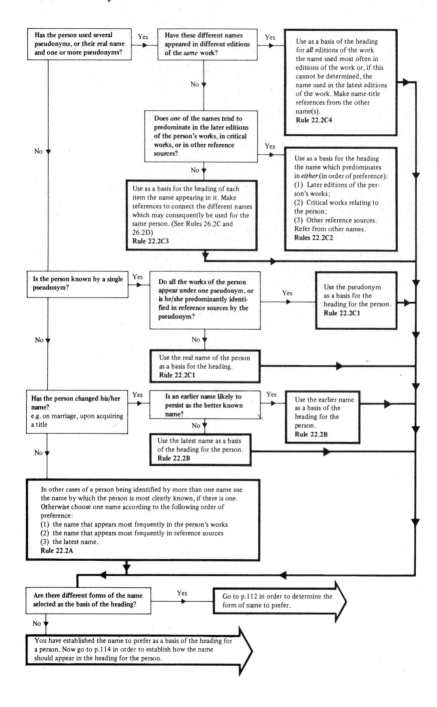

Has the person used several pseudonyms, or their real name and one or more pseudonyms? — Yes → Have these different names appeared in different editions of the *same* work? — Yes → Use as a basis of the heading for *all* editions of the work the name used most often in editions of the work or, if this cannot be determined, the name used in the latest editions of the work. Make name-title references from the other name(s). **Rule 22.2C4**

No ↓

Does *one* of the names tend to predominate in the later editions of the person's works, in critical works, or in other reference sources? — Yes → Use as a basis for the heading the name which predominates in *either* (in order of preference): (1) Later editions of the person's works; (2) Critical works relating to the person; (3) Other reference sources. Refer from other names. **Rules 22.2C2**

No ↓

Use as a basis for the heading of each item the name appearing in it. Make references to connect the different names which may consequently be used for the same person. (See Rules 26.2C and 26.2D) **Rule 22.2C3**

No ↓

Is the person known by a single pseudonym? — Yes → Do all the works of the person appear under one pseudonym, or is he/she predominantly identified in reference sources by the pseudonym? — Yes → Use the pseudonym as a basis for the heading for the person. **Rule 22.2C1**

No ↓   No ↓

Use the real name of the person as a basis for the heading. **Rule 22.2C1**

Has the person changed his/her name? e.g. on marriage, upon acquiring a title — Yes → Is an earlier name likely to persist as the better known name? — Yes → Use the earlier name as a basis of the heading for the person. **Rule 22.2B**

No ↓

Use the latest name as a basis of the heading for the person. **Rule 22.2B**

No ↓

In other cases of a person being identified by more than one name use the name by which the person is most clearly known, if there is one. Otherwise choose one name according to the following order of preference:
(1) the name that appears most frequently in the person's works
(2) the name that appears most frequently in reference sources
(3) the latest name.
Rule 22.2A

Are there different forms of the name selected as the basis of the heading? — Yes → Go to p.112 in order to determine the form of name to prefer.

No ↓

You have established the name to prefer as a basis of the heading for a person. Now go to p.114 in order to establish how the name should appear in the heading for the person.

You have arrived here by deciding that:
An entry under the name of a PERSON is required and that the person is or has been known by DIFFERENT FORMS of the same name.

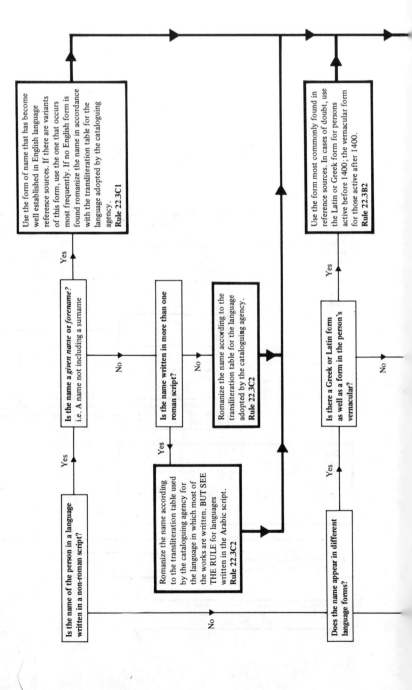

Is the name of the person in a language written in a non-roman script?

Yes →

Is the name a *given name* or *forename*? i.e. A name not including a surname

Yes →

Use the form of name that has become well established in English language reference sources. If there are variants of this form, use the one that occurs most frequently. If no English form is found romanize the name in accordance with the transliteration table for the language adopted by the cataloguing agency.
Rule 22.3C1

No ↓

Is the name written in more than one roman script?

Yes →

Romanize the name according to the transliteration table used by the cataloguing agency for the language in which most of the works are written. BUT SEE THE RULE for languages written in the Arabic script.
Rule 22.3C2

No →

Romanize the name according to the transliteration table for the language adopted by the cataloguing agency.
Rule 22.3C2

No ↓

Does the name appear in different language forms?

Yes →

Is there a Greek or Latin form as well as a form in the person's vernacular?

Yes →

Use the form most commonly found in reference sources. In cases of doubt, use the Latin or Greek form for persons active before 1400; the vernacular form for those active after 1400.
Rule 22.3B2

No →

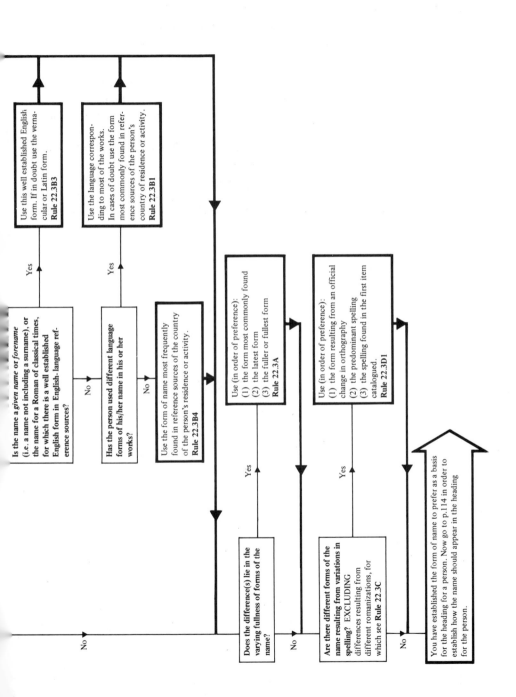

Is the name a *given name* or *forename* (i.e. a name not including a surname), or the name for a Roman of classical times, for which there is a well established English form in English-language reference sources?

Yes → Use this well established English form. If in doubt use the vernacular or Latin form. **Rule 22.3B3**

No ↓

Has the person used **different language forms** of his/her name in his or her works?

Yes → Use the language corresponding to most of the works. In cases of doubt use the form most commonly found in reference sources of the person's country of residence or activity. **Rule 22.3B1**

No ↓

Use the form of name most frequently found in reference sources of the country of the person's residence or activity. **Rule 22.3B4**

Does the difference(s) lie in the varying fullness of forms of the name?

Yes → Use (in order of preference):
(1) the form most commonly found
(2) the latest form
(3) the fuller or fullest form
Rule 22.3A

No ↓

Are there different forms of the name resulting from variations in spelling? EXCLUDING differences resulting from different romanizations, for which see **Rule 22.3C**

Yes → Use (in order of preference):
(1) the form resulting from an official change in orthography
(2) the predominant spelling
(3) the spelling found in the first item catalogued.
Rule 22.3D1

No ↓

You have established the form of name to prefer as a basis for the heading for a person. Now go to p.114 in order to establish how the name should appear in the heading for the person.

You have arrived here by deciding that:

An entry under the name of a PERSON is required. You have chosen the basis for the heading, and now need to establish the way in which the name will appear in the heading. The form and usage of names in non-Western cultures may be unfamiliar. Therefore, special rules are provided for names in certain foreign languages: these indicate the entry element for such names, and their structure in a heading.

Note

(1) Whilst these special rules will generally be self-sufficient in handling names in the languages to which they relate, occasionally it may be necessary to refer to the general rules in chapter 22 (or to the appropriate point in the algorithm dealing with this chapter).

(2) In particular, Rules 22.18-22.19 (p.125 of the algorithm) will apply if it is necessary to distinguish between identical names.

(3) Much more comprehensive and detailed guidance on the handling of personal names is given in — *Names of persons: national usages for entry in catalogues,* compiled by the IFLA Office for UBC. 3rd ed. London, The Office, 1977.

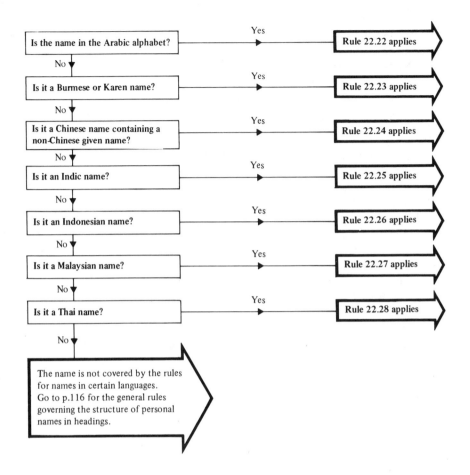

Is the name in the Arabic alphabet? — Yes → Rule 22.22 applies

No ↓

Is it a Burmese or Karen name? — Yes → Rule 22.23 applies

No ↓

Is it a Chinese name containing a non-Chinese given name? — Yes → Rule 22.24 applies

No ↓

Is it an Indic name? — Yes → Rule 22.25 applies

No ↓

Is it an Indonesian name? — Yes → Rule 22.26 applies

No ↓

Is it a Malaysian name? — Yes → Rule 22.27 applies

No ↓

Is it a Thai name? — Yes → Rule 22.28 applies

No ↓

The name is not covered by the rules for names in certain languages.
Go to p.116 for the general rules governing the structure of personal names in headings.

You have arrived here by deciding that:

An entry under the name of a PERSON is required. You have selected the name to be used as the basis of the heading for the person. You now need to determine HOW the name should appear in the heading: notably, to establish what the *entry element* will be. In addition, you have decided that the name is not covered by the special rules for names in certain languages which are listed on p.114 of this algorithm.

Note

(1) If a person's name consists of several parts, select as entry element that part of the name under which the person would normally be listed in authoritative alphabetic lists in his or her language or country. **Rule 22.4A**

(2) Rules 22.5-22.9 (to which the next section of the algorithm relates) conform to and support this general ruling. If, however, a person's known preference conflicts with the Rules, follow that preference. **Rule 22.4A**

(3) If the entry element is the first element of the name, enter the name in direct order. e.g. Ram Gopal. **Rule 22.4B1**

(4) If the first element is a surname, follow it by a comma. e.g. Name – Foo Kwac Wah: Foo being the surname. Heading takes the form – Foo, Kwac Wah. **Rule 22.4B2**

(5) If the entry element is not the first element of the name, transpose the elements of the name preceding the entry element. Follow the entry element by a comma. e.g. Name – John Doe. Heading takes the form – Doe, John. **Rule 22.4B3**

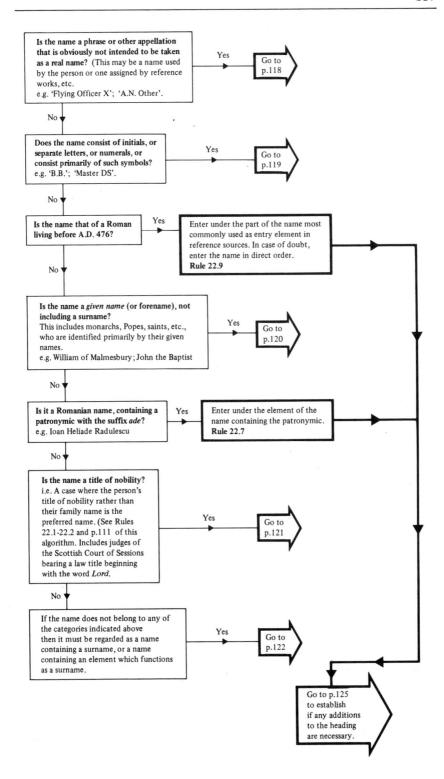

Is the name a phrase or other appellation that is obviously not intended to be taken as a real name? (This may be a name used by the person or one assigned by reference works, etc.
e.g. 'Flying Officer X'; 'A.N. Other'.

Yes → Go to p.118

No ↓

Does the name consist of initials, or separate letters, or numerals, or consist primarily of such symbols?
e.g. 'B.B.'; 'Master DS'.

Yes → Go to p.119

No ↓

Is the name that of a Roman living before A.D. 476?

Yes → Enter under the part of the name most commonly used as entry element in reference sources. In case of doubt, enter the name in direct order. **Rule 22.9**

No ↓

Is the name a *given name* (or forename), not including a surname?
This includes monarchs, Popes, saints, etc., who are identified primarily by their given names.
e.g. William of Malmesbury; John the Baptist

Yes → Go to p.120

No ↓

Is it a Romanian name, containing a patronymic with the suffix *ade*?
e.g. Ioan Heliade Radulescu

Yes → Enter under the element of the name containing the patronymic. **Rule 22.7**

No ↓

Is the name a title of nobility?
i.e. A case where the person's title of nobility rather than their family name is the preferred name. (See Rules 22.1-22.2 and p.111 of this algorithm. Includes judges of the Scottish Court of Sessions bearing a law title beginning with the word *Lord*.

Yes → Go to p.121

No ↓

If the name does not belong to any of the categories indicated above then it must be regarded as a name containing a surname, or a name containing an element which functions as a surname.

Yes → Go to p.122

Go to p.125 to establish if any additions to the heading are necessary.

You have arrived here by deciding that:

An entry under the name of a PERSON is required and that the name consists of a PHRASE (or other appellation obviously not intended to be taken as a real name).

Note

Where such a phrase, etc., is used as a heading and it does not convey the idea of a person, add a suitable designation in English. e.g. River (Writer); Taj Mahal (Musician).

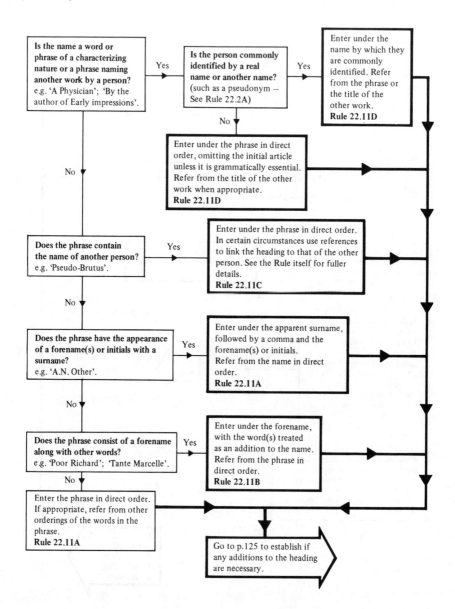

You have arrived here by deciding that:

An entry under the name of a PERSON is required and that the name consists of INITIALS, or SEPARATE LETTERS, or NUMERALS, or consists primarily of such symbols.

Note

Identifications consisting of predominantly non-alphabetic or non-numeric devices (e.g. @@??@@; or M@@@) are not regarded as names. Works whose authorship is indicated only in this way are entered under title. *See* **Rule 21.5C.**

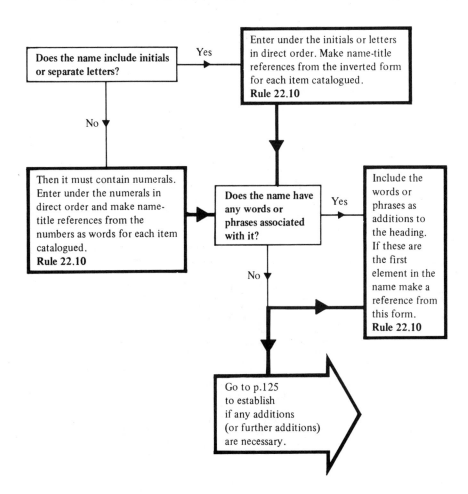

You have arrived here by deciding that:
An entry under the name of a PERSON is required and that the name is a GIVEN name.

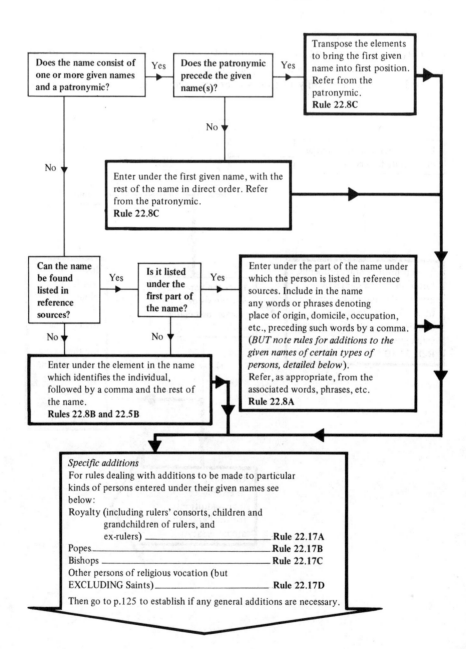

Does the name consist of one or more given names and a patronymic? — Yes → **Does the patronymic precede the given name(s)?** — Yes → Transpose the elements to bring the first given name into first position. Refer from the patronymic. **Rule 22.8C**

No ↓ (from "Does the patronymic precede")

Enter under the first given name, with the rest of the name in direct order. Refer from the patronymic. **Rule 22.8C**

No ↓ (from "Does the name consist")

Can the name be found listed in reference sources? — Yes → **Is it listed under the first part of the name?** — Yes → Enter under the part of the name under which the person is listed in reference sources. Include in the name any words or phrases denoting place of origin, domicile, occupation, etc., preceding such words by a comma. (*BUT note rules for additions to the given names of certain types of persons, detailed below*). Refer, as appropriate, from the associated words, phrases, etc. **Rule 22.8A**

No ↓ (from "Can the name be found")

No ↓ (from "Is it listed")

Enter under the element in the name which identifies the individual, followed by a comma and the rest of the name. **Rules 22.8B and 22.5B**

Specific additions
For rules dealing with additions to be made to particular kinds of persons entered under their given names see below:
Royalty (including rulers' consorts, children and grandchildren of rulers, and ex-rulers) _____ **Rule 22.17A**
Popes _____ **Rule 22.17B**
Bishops _____ **Rule 22.17C**
Other persons of religious vocation (but EXCLUDING Saints) _____ **Rule 22.17D**
Then go to p.125 to establish if any general additions are necessary.

You have arrived here by deciding that:

An entry under the name of a PERSON is required and that the name is a title of nobility (including judges of the Scottish Court of Sessions bearing a law title beginning with the word *Lord*).

Note

This section of the algorithm applies only to cases where the title (rather than the family name) has been established as the preferred name for the person. See Rules 22.1-22.2 and p.111 of the algorithm.

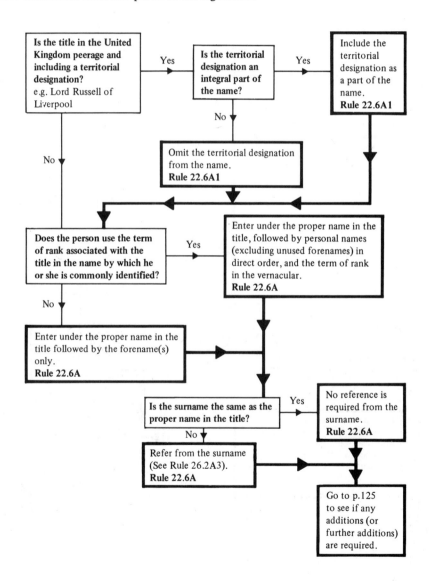

You have arrived here by deciding that:
An entry under the name of a PERSON is required and that the name contains a SURNAME or an element FUNCTIONING AS A SURNAME.

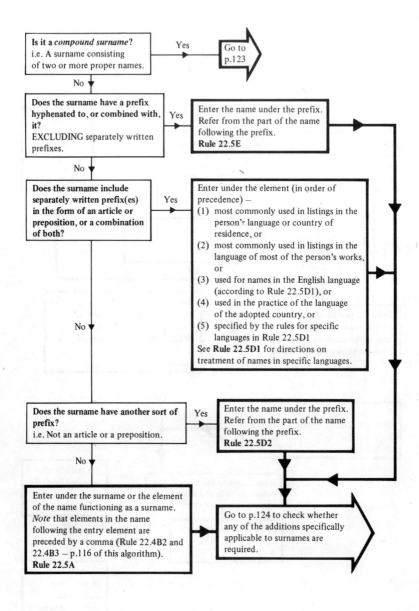

You have arrived here by deciding that:

An entry under the name of a PERSON is required and that you are dealing with a COMPOUND SURNAME.

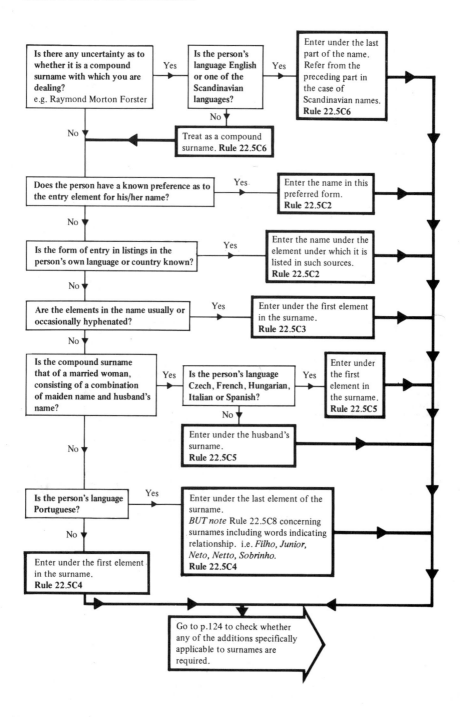

Is there any uncertainty as to whether it is a compound surname with which you are dealing?
e.g. Raymond Morton Forster

Yes → Is the person's language English or one of the Scandinavian languages?

Yes → Enter under the last part of the name. Refer from the preceding part in the case of Scandinavian names. **Rule 22.5C6**

No ↓

Treat as a compound surname. **Rule 22.5C6**

No ↓

Does the person have a known preference as to the entry element for his/her name?

Yes → Enter the name in this preferred form. **Rule 22.5C2**

No ↓

Is the form of entry in listings in the person's own language or country known?

Yes → Enter the name under the element under which it is listed in such sources. **Rule 22.5C2**

No ↓

Are the elements in the name usually or occasionally hyphenated?

Yes → Enter under the first element in the surname. **Rule 22.5C3**

No ↓

Is the compound surname that of a married woman, consisting of a combination of maiden name and husband's name?

Yes → Is the person's language Czech, French, Hungarian, Italian or Spanish?

Yes → Enter under the first element in the surname. **Rule 22.5C5**

No ↓

Enter under the husband's surname. **Rule 22.5C5**

No ↓

Is the person's language Portuguese?

Yes → Enter under the last element of the surname. *BUT note* Rule 22.5C8 concerning surnames including words indicating relationship. i.e. *Filho, Junior, Neto, Netto, Sobrinho.* **Rule 22.5C4**

No ↓

Enter under the first element in the surname. **Rule 22.5C4**

Go to p.124 to check whether any of the additions specifically applicable to surnames are required.

You have arrived here to decide about ADDITIONS which may be required specifically for the headings of PERSONS entered under their SURNAME.

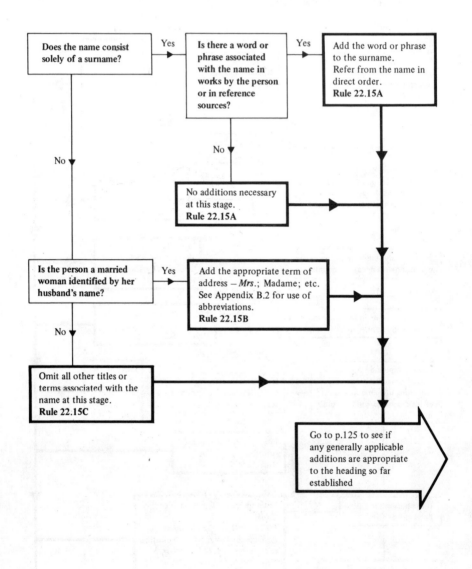

Does the name consist solely of a surname?

Yes → Is there a word or phrase associated with the name in works by the person or in reference sources?

Yes → Add the word or phrase to the surname. Refer from the name in direct order. **Rule 22.15A**

No

No → No additions necessary at this stage. **Rule 22.15A**

Is the person a married woman identified by her husband's name?

Yes → Add the appropriate term of address — *Mrs.*; Madame; etc. See Appendix B.2 for use of abbreviations. **Rule 22.15B**

No

Omit all other titles or terms associated with the name at this stage. **Rule 22.15C**

Go to p.125 to see if any generally applicable additions are appropriate to the heading so far established

You have arrived here to decide about ADDITIONS which may be generally applicable to headings for PERSONS.

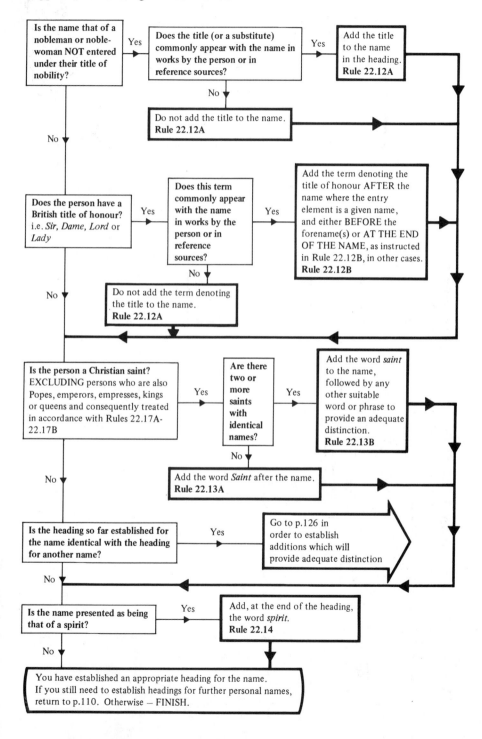

Is the name that of a nobleman or noblewoman NOT entered under their title of nobility? — Yes → **Does the title (or a substitute) commonly appear with the name in works by the person or in reference sources?** — Yes → Add the title to the name in the heading. **Rule 22.12A**

No ↓ (from title question): Do not add the title to the name. **Rule 22.12A**

No ↓

Does the person have a British title of honour? i.e. *Sir, Dame, Lord* or *Lady* — Yes → **Does this term commonly appear with the name in works by the person or in reference sources?** — Yes → Add the term denoting the title of honour AFTER the name where the entry element is a given name, and either BEFORE the forename(s) or AT THE END OF THE NAME, as instructed in Rule 22.12B, in other cases. **Rule 22.12B**

No ↓ (from term question): Do not add the term denoting the title to the name. **Rule 22.12A**

No ↓

Is the person a Christian saint? EXCLUDING persons who are also Popes, emperors, empresses, kings or queens and consequently treated in accordance with Rules 22.17A-22.17B — Yes → **Are there two or more saints with identical names?** — Yes → Add the word *saint* to the name, followed by any other suitable word or phrase to provide an adequate distinction. **Rule 22.13B**

No ↓ (from saints question): Add the word *Saint* after the name. **Rule 22.13A**

No ↓

Is the heading so far established for the name identical with the heading for another name? — Yes → Go to p.126 in order to establish additions which will provide adequate distinction

No ↓

Is the name presented as being that of a spirit? — Yes → Add, at the end of the heading, the word *spirit*. **Rule 22.14**

No ↓

You have established an appropriate heading for the name. If you still need to establish headings for further personal names, return to p.110. Otherwise – FINISH.

You have arrived here to decide the **ADDITIONS** which you should make in order to distinguish the heading for the name of a PERSON which is IDENTICAL with the heading for another person.

Is part or all of the name represented by initials?

Yes →

Is the full form of the name known?

No

Yes →

Does the name consist entirely of initials?

No →

Yes →

Add the full form of the name at the end of the name. **Rule 22.16A**

Are the initials a part of the entry element?

No →

Yes →

Add the full form of the entry element at the end of the name. **Rule 22.16A**

Add the full form of the inverted part of the name (forenames, etc.) at the end of the name. **Rule 22.16A**

Is the name now distinguished from otherwise identical names?

Yes →

No

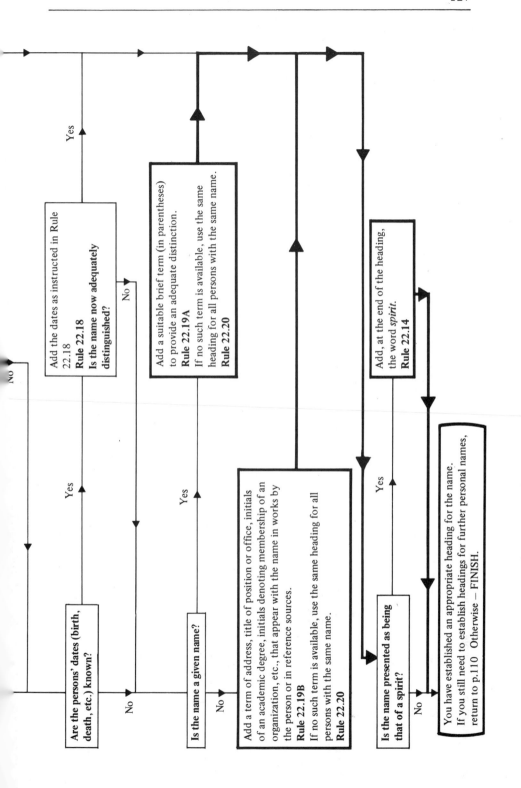

No — Yes

Are the persons' dates (birth, death, etc.) known?

Yes — Add the dates as instructed in Rule 22.18
Rule 22.18
Is the name now adequately distinguished?
No

No — **Is the name a given name?**

Yes — Add a suitable brief term (in parentheses) to provide an adequate distinction.
Rule 22.19A
If no such term is available, use the same heading for all persons with the same name.
Rule 22.20

No — Add a term of address, title of position or office, initials of an academic degree, initials denoting membership of an organization, etc., that appear with the name in works by the person or in reference sources.
Rule 22.19B
If no such term is available, use the same heading for all persons with the same name.
Rule 22.20

Is the name presented as being that of a spirit?

Yes — Add, at the end of the heading, the word *spirit*.
Rule 22.14

No — You have established an appropriate heading for the name.
If you still need to establish headings for further personal names, return to p.110   Otherwise — FINISH.

Algorithm 1 : complete structure

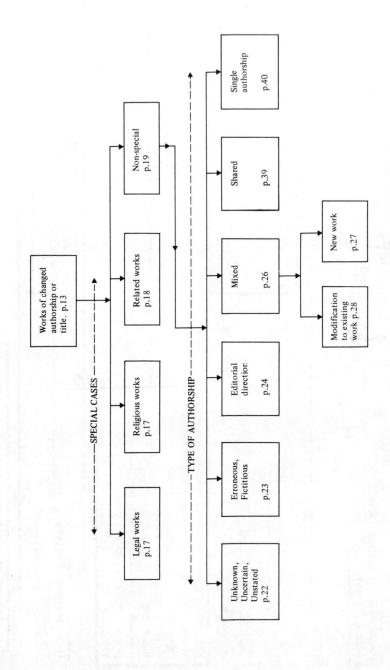

Algorithm 2 : complete structure

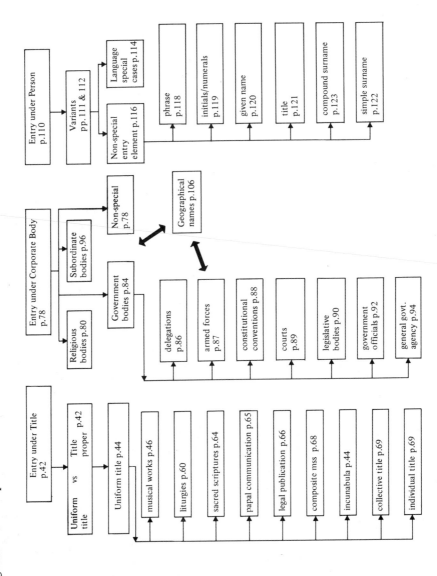

Introduction to the worked examples

Please read the following notes carefully before attempting the excercises.

The specimen items that are included in this final part are a graduated practice in the application of both algorithm and code. Data for author cataloguing decisions is given in the form of facsimiles of title-pages, with further information as appropriate. These follow this introduction, solutions being given at the end of the book. The practical work has been divided into three sections:

Section 1, covering examples 1-16. At the outset these should be considered in terms of part one of the algorithm only (chapter 21 of the code). Thus one approach should be selected as the main entry in each case, and the features requiring added entries identified. There is no need to construct actual headings. The solutions therefore merely indicate the approaches to be covered with reference to the appropriate rules from chapter 21.

Section 2, covering examples 17-32. For these the complete author cataloguing can be undertaken with construction of headings for all entries and the provision of supporting references as required. Solutions are given under the term 'Headings', the main entry being quoted first in all cases.

Section 3, covering headings for items 1-16. These are listed at the end so as to complete the author cataloguing for all items used.

For section 1 the appropriate rules from chapter 21 are listed for all entries in each case. Added entries are dealt with in the code by supplementary notes to rules for main entry as well as by two separate rules at the end of the chapter, but we have considered it convenient to refer to the latter in all instances as far as possible. For section 2 where the emphasis is on the ensuing chapters reference to chapter 21 is more selective and largely confined to problems not previously exemplified.

Certain points connected with the formulation of (in particular) personal names raise difficulties for an exercise based on the examination of a single title-page per item. These have to do with, for instance, selection of a predominant form of name or a decision about the use of initials as against full forenames i.e. situations where the cataloguer in a working context would draw on a wider range of data than is provided here. Our approach has been to give extra information about variant forms of an author's name in one or two examples where it is wished to highlight problems of this kind. For all other items the form used on the title-page should be assumed to be the basis of the entry.

EXAMPLE 1   *133*

Pan Piper Science Series

COMPUTERS

K. N. DODD

A PAN ORIGINAL

PAN BOOKS LTD : LONDON

THE OBSERVER'S BOOK OF

WILD ANIMALS

OF THE BRITISH ISLES

Compiled by

W. J. STOKOE

Revised by

MAURICE BURTON, D.Sc.

Describing
SIXTY-FOUR SPECIES
with 72 illustrations
46 of which are in full colour

FREDERICK WARNE & CO. LTD.
FREDERICK WARNE & CO. INC.
LONDON · NEW YORK

'This edition stands very much as compiled by Mr W.J. Stokoe' (Preface) – 'The Observer's Pocket Series' (half-title).

EXAMPLE 3   135

EIGIL KIAER

GARDEN
FLOWERS

IN COLOUR

Illustrated by
VERNER HANCKE

Translated by
H. G. WITHAM FOGG

BLANDFORD PRESS
LONDON

Originally published in Denmark as 'Havens Blomster I Farver'.

WILD FLOWERS

OF THE

WAYSIDE AND WOODLAND

COMPILED BY

T. H. SCOTT AND W. J. STOKOE

BASED UPON THE STANDARD WORK
"WAYSIDE & WOODLAND BLOSSOMS"
BY EDWARD STEP, F.L.S.

CONTAINING

A DESCRIPTIVE HISTORY OF 762 SPECIES

TOGETHER WITH

EIGHTY PLATES IN COLOUR

ILLUSTRATING

THREE HUNDRED AND TWENTY
BLOSSOMS AND LEAVES

ALSO

A PICTORIAL COLOUR KEY
TO FACILITATE IDENTIFICATION

FREDERICK WARNE & CO., LTD,

LONDON & NEW YORK

The preface describes Step's original work as the 'foundation' for the present one and indicates that the original illustrations have been retained. 'Wayside and woodland blossoms' was published in two series 1895/96 with a third series in 1929.

EXAMPLE 5 *137*

DRAWINGS
BY PISANELLO

A SELECTION
WITH INTRODUCTION & NOTES

BY GEORGE F. HILL
LATE KEEPER OF COINS AND MEDALS, BRITISH MUSEUM

DOVER PUBLICATIONS, INC., NEW YORK

The textual material, consisting of a short introduction followed by notes on the individual plates occupies about half the book. Antonio Pisanello is the name by which Antonio di Bartolommeo Pisano has come to be known.

BLACKWELL'S FRENCH TEXTS

General Editor : ALFRED EWERT

VOLTAIRE
Lettres Philosophiques

Edited by
F. A. TAYLOR
SOMETIME STUDENT OF
CHRIST CHURCH, OXFORD

BASIL BLACKWELL · OXFORD
1965

A collection of Voltaire's letters in the original French and designed to provide an authentic text. Taylor contributes an introduction and critical notes to the letters. Voltaire was the pseudonym of François-Marie Arouet.

EXAMPLE 7 *139*

MODERN STUDIES IN PHILOSOPHY

DESCARTES

A Collection of Critical Essays

EDITED BY WILLIS DONEY

MACMILLAN

LONDON . MELBOURNE

1968

Contains 16 essays by various authors, mostly reprints of articles in specialist journals. Modern Studies in Philosophy is a series of such anthologies dealing with individual philosophers.

THE COUPLE

A Sexual Profile by Mr. and Mrs. K

As Told to Monte Ghertler and Alfred Palca

W. H. ALLEN

A Division of Howard & Wyndham Ltd

1972

The work is narrated in the first person by Harold and Joan (the couple) — 'our book is based on our memory of events' (i.e. of sex therapy at a St. Louis sex clinic).

EXAMPLE 9   *141*

THE LIMITS TO GROWTH

A REPORT FOR
THE CLUB OF ROME'S PROJECT ON
THE PREDICAMENT OF MANKIND

Donella H. Meadows

Dennis L. Meadows

Jørgen Randers

William W. Behrens III

A Potomac Associates Book
EARTH ISLAND LIMITED, LONDON

The Club of Rome is an informal international organization, the aim of its project being to 'examine the complex of problems troubling the men of all nations'. The individuals named on the title-page were members of a research team at the Massachusetts Institute of Technology, whose findings (based on computer studies) form the basis of the book. Dennis Meadows was the director of the research, which received financial support from the Volkswagen Foundation.

Report of the Tropical Products Institute 1972-74

Director P.C.Spensley, MA, BSc, DPhil, FRIC

Editors Melba Kershaw J.B.Davis

London 1974

The Institute is a scientific unit of the Ministry of Overseas Development. The report covers the work of the unit and the director appears to be the nominal author of the greater part of it.

EXAMPLE 11   *143*

THE
DIRECTORY
OF
SUMMER JOBS
IN
BRITAIN

1972 EDITION

Editor:

Sally E. Moon

Published annually by

VACATION-WORK
9 Park End Street, Oxford

The openings listed are the result of research done by Vacation-Work.

MINISTRY OF PUBLIC BUILDING AND WORKS
ANCIENT MONUMENTS AND HISTORIC BUILDINGS

Stonehenge

WILTSHIRE

by

R. S. NEWALL, F.S.A.

LONDON
HER MAJESTY'S STATIONERY OFFICE
1959

'Ancient Monuments and Historic Buildings' refers to a section of the Ministry. It now ranks as a division of the Department of the Environment.

EXAMPLE 13   *145*

National Parks Commission
COASTAL PRESERVATION AND DEVELOPMENT
A study of the coastline of England and Wales

The Coasts of Yorkshire and Lincolnshire

*Report of the Regional Coastal Conference
held at York on February 14th, 1967*

LONDON

HER MAJESTY'S STATIONERY OFFICE: 1968

One of a series of documents with the title 'Coastal Preservation and Development', each being concerned with the coastline of a particular part of the country and resulting from a regional conference. The National Parks Commission was superseded by the Countryside Commission in 1968.

SOME SAYINGS OF THE BUDDHA
ACCORDING TO THE PĀLI CANON

Translated by
F. L. WOODWARD

With an Introduction by
SIR FRANCIS YOUNGHUSBAND

LONDON
OXFORD UNIVERSITY PRESS

Pali is a dead language related to Sanskrit. Younghusband's introduction occupies about 12 pages. The work consists of selections from various parts of the Canon.

EXAMPLE 15 *147*

NEW ENGLISH BIBLE

NEW TESTAMENT

c
o
n
c
o
r
d
a
n
c
e

COMPILED BY E. ELDER

MARSHALL MORGAN & SCOTT Ltd

LONDON · EDINBURGH

ENCYCLICAL LETTER
(POPULORUM PROGRESSIO)

of
His Holiness

PAUL VI

by Divine Providence

POPE

To the Bishops,
Priests, Religious, the
Faithful of the whole Catholic world,
and to all men of good will,
on

FOSTERING THE DEVELOPMENT
OF PEOPLES

LONDON
CATHOLIC TRUTH SOCIETY
PUBLISHERS TO THE HOLY SEE

The encyclical is translated from the Latin. The Catholic Truth Society is concerned with assisting 'all Catholics to a better knowledge of their religion', and with propagation generally. The cover reads 'The Great/social problem/Encyclical Letter of Pope Paul VI/'Populorum Progressio'/1967.' Pope Paul's pontificate lasted from 1963-78.

EXAMPLE 17 *149*

THE LOGIC OF SCIENTIFIC DISCOVERY

KARL R. POPPER

HUTCHINSON OF LONDON

Karl Raimund Popper was knighted in 1964, but the form quoted on the above title-page appears to be the most commonly used, both before and after his knighthood.

DRS. F.J.J. VAN BAARS
DRS. J.G.J. A. VAN DER SCHOOT

ENGELS
NEDERLANDS
WOORDENBOEK

UITGEVERIJ HET SPECTRUM N.V.
UTRECHT/ANTWERPEN

An English-Dutch dictionary. Drs is an academic title and should be disregarded.

EXAMPLE 19   *151*

Mao Tse-tung

An Anthology of His Writings

EDITED WITH AN INTRODUCTION BY
ANNE FREMANTLE

A MENTOR BOOK
Published by
The New American Library, New York and Toronto
The New English Library Limited, London

Fremantle contributes a 40 page introduction but there is no commentary. Mao is a family name. i.e. For the purposes of the exercise the equivalent of a western surname.

THE
NOTEBOOKS
OF
LEONARDO
DA VINCI

A NEW SELECTION BY PAMELA TAYLOR

A Mentor Classic Published by
The New American Library

Taylor contributes a general introduction and brief notes at the beginning
of the various sections. Da Vinci is not a surname.

EXAMPLE 21   *153*

Antonia Fraser

Quiet as a Nun

Penguin Books

Daughter of the 7th Earl of Longford, the author was Lady Antonia Pakenham until her marriage in 1956, when she became Lady Antonia Fraser. She wrote one or two books as Antonia Pakenham and the rest as Antonia Fraser, in neither case using her title.

Spon's Mechanical and Electrical Services Price Book

EDITED BY
DAVIS, BELFIELD & EVEREST
Chartered Quantity Surveyors

1971

Second Edition

E. & F. N. SPON LTD
11 NEW FETTER LANE · LONDON EC4

Brings together an assortment of facts about wage rates, materials prices, estimating, fees etc.

EXAMPLE 23   *155*

SCIENCE MUSEUM
LONDON

A Brief History of Flying

from Myth to Space Travel

by

CHARLES HARVARD GIBBS-SMITH

M.A. (Harvard); Honorary Companion of
the Royal Aeronautical Society

LONDON
HER MAJESTY'S STATIONERY OFFICE
1967

The Science Museum is a government institution.

DEPARTMENT OF EDUCATION AND SCIENCE

Library Advisory Council (England)
Library Advisory Council (Wales)

A REPORT
ON THE SUPPLY AND TRAINING
OF LIBRARIANS

LONDON
HER MAJESTY'S STATIONERY OFFICE
1968

'... it shall be the duty of each Council to advise the Secretary of State upon such matters connected with the provision or use of library facilities.' (Public Libraries and Museums Act 1964)

EXAMPLE 25   157

A Framework for Government Research and Development

Presented to Parliament by
The Lord Privy Seal
by Command of Her Majesty
November 1971

LONDON
HER MAJESTY'S STATIONERY OFFICE
52½p net

Cmnd. 4814

The document is a government green paper combining two reports on science policy, the first by Lord Rothschild, Head of the Central Policy Review Staff, the second by the Council for Scientific Policy. The full name and title of Lord Rothschild (so described in the report) is Nathaniel Mayer Victor Rothschild, 3rd Baron Rothschild. The document is often referred to as the Rothschild Report. The Council for Scientific Policy is a government advisory body. Treat the item as a single policy document, using the additional information supplied to determine secondary access points.

The composer's full name is Claude-Achille Debussy. The record contains
the complete work, the first two movements being listed on the side shown.

EXAMPLE 27   *159*

THE PENGUIN BOOK OF

English Folk Songs

FROM THE

JOURNAL OF THE FOLK SONG SOCIETY

AND THE

JOURNAL OF THE ENGLISH FOLK DANCE AND SONG SOCIETY

*

SELECTED AND EDITED BY

R. Vaughan Williams & A. L. Lloyd

*

PENGUIN BOOKS

The document includes both words and music, the editors having preserved both in their original form, except for the collating of different versions of the lyrics in a few cases. The Folk Song Society became the English Folk Dance and Song Society in the early 1900s, with a corresponding change in the name of the journal. The name Vaughan Williams is usually regarded as compound and some reference sources hyphenate it.

THE
NEW ENGLISH
BIBLE

NEW TESTAMENT

OXFORD UNIVERSITY PRESS
CAMBRIDGE UNIVERSITY PRESS

1961

EXAMPLE 29   *161*

ALICE'S ADVENTURES IN WONDERLAND

THROUGH THE LOOKING-GLASS AND OTHER WRITINGS

LEWIS CARROLL

With an Introduction by
ROBIN DENNISTON
Illustrations copied from Tenniel by
DOROTHY COLLES

COLLINS
LONDON AND GLASGOW

The author's real name was Charles Lutwidge Dodgson under which he wrote various mathematical works. The 'other writings' mentioned in the title are minor and should be disregarded for this exercise.

Sir Isaac Newton's

MATHEMATICAL
PRINCIPLES

OF NATURAL PHILOSOPHY AND HIS
SYSTEM OF THE WORLD

Translated into English by Andrew Motte in 1729.
The translations revised, and supplied with an
historical and explanatory appendix, by

FLORIAN CAJORI

UNIVERSITY OF CALIFORNIA PRESS
BERKELEY AND LOS ANGELES
1962

Originally published in Latin in 1687 as 'Philosophiae Naturalis Principia
Mathematica', and usually referred to by the shortened form 'Principia
Mathematica'. One other translation into English exists, though only of
part of the work. Cajori's appendix occupies over 50 pages.

EXAMPLE 31   *163*

In 4 volumes

J. D. Bernal

Science in History

Volume 2: The Scientific and Industrial Revolutions

106 illustrations

Penguin Books

THE THEFT ACT
1968

By

EDWARD GRIEW, M.A., LL.B.

of Gray's Inn, Barrister-at-Law,
Senior Lecturer in Law at the
University of Leicester

LONDON
SWEET & MAXWELL
1968

The bulk of the work is a commentary on the Act, which also contains however the complete text in the form of an appendix. Headings should be constructed with this fact in mind.

Solutions and commentaries on examples

SECTION 1

For examples 1-16, using part 1 of the algorithm to determine access points only. The actual headings for these items will be given in section 3.

Example 1

Main entry
> under Dodd, a typical case of single personal authorship involving rule **21.4A**

Added entries
> (1) The title of the series, by **21.30L**
> (2) The title of the document, but not in the case of a dictionary catalogue, where 'computers' would almost certainly occur either as a subject heading or as a subject reference, by rule **21.30J(3)**

The lengthy procedure required to determine a main entry which is intuitively obvious for this first item arises because the purpose of the charts is to arrive at decisions systematically by a process of elimination. The student can easily dismiss change of title as not relevant and recognize that the work does not belong to any of the categories treated as 'special', and that it is not related to another document in any intrinsic way. The definitions of authorship then lead on to the principal conditions of authorship of which the final one i.e. single authorship is seen to be appropriate. Following the direction to the section covering choice between various situations of single corporate or personal authorship the latter is selected and the final box indicates the rule cited above.

Example 2

Main entry
> under the original author i.e. Stokoe, by **21.12A**

Added entries
> (1) The reviser i.e. Burton, by **21.29B**
> (2) The title of the document, by **21.30J**

The series entry is omitted by reference to **21.30L(1)**, but note that it is in any case redundant since the title entries for this series effectively bring the items together in the file.

The algorithm leads through mixed authorship via modification of another work in the form of a printed text to revisions.

Example 3

Main entry

under Kiaer as author of the original work by **21.14A** (i.e. not under the translator) and as writer of the text by **21.11A** (i.e. not under the illustrator)

Added entries
 (1) The illustrator i.e. under Hancke, by **21.30K2(a)**
 (2) The title of the document, by **21.30J**

An added entry for the translator is rejected on the grounds that it does not clearly meet any of the criteria laid down in **21.30K1**. Of these (b) and (c) are hard to establish but are likely to apply mainly to works of a literary nature. The others are not relevant.

The algorithm must be consulted twice to resolve the preference of author over illustrator and translator respectively, but in both cases the route leads through mixed authorship to modification of another work in the form of a printed text. It is not impossible that the order in which the decisions were made in such a case might affect the outcome but since there are no situations in which either of the added entry features would be preferred to the author there is no problem with this example.

Example 4

Main entry

under the first compiler i.e. Scott, by **21.12B** and **21.6C1**

Added entries
 (1) The second compiler i.e. Stokoe, by **21.30B**
 (2) The original author i.e. Step, by **21.29B**
 (3) The title of the document, by **21.30J**

21.12B requires entry under the reviser when 'the person or body responsible for the original is no longer considered to be responsible for the work', but also requires the decision to be made by reference to the chief source of information i.e. the title-page (in the case of a book), a rather unhelpful restriction. The preferred solution therefore rests on the somewhat slender evidence of the phrase 'based on' and the fact that Scott and Stokoe **are** named first on the title-page. The change of title may be significant too, **though** this is a rather unreliable criterion. The further decision as between Scott and Stokoe is a simple one involving shared authorship.

Example 5

Main entry
> under the artist i.e. Pisanello, by **21.17B**. This is a flexible rule allowing the cataloguer to use his discretion according to the varying importance of the textual material in different works of this nature. Here the words 'with introduction & notes by' is taken to imply that Hill is not 'represented as the author of the work'. (In any case the artist is preferred in 'doubtful cases').

Added entries
> (1) The writer of the text, by **21.30C**
> (2) The title of the document, by **21.30J**

This item can usefully be compared with example 3, both being 'modifications'. In this case however the modification is of an art work since the drawings clearly precede the book. The student's attention is drawn to a third category of pictorial matter with text, namely that in which artist and author are in genuine collaboration with no obvious order of dependence as between the two elements of the work. This is arrived at via the 'collaborative new works' box which represents the second of the two primary definitions of mixed authorship.

Example 6

Main entry
> under the letter writer i.e. Voltaire, by **21.15B**

Added entries
> (1) The editor i.e. Taylor, by **21.30D**. Note that this rule refers to 'monographic works'. Series editors can be ignored.
> (2) The title of the series, by **21.30L**
> (3) The title of the document, by **21.30J**

If title entry via 21.7 has been arrived at the definition of collection should be checked. In fact this is another case of the modification of a work in the form of a printed text and, more specifically, it is a text with critical material.

Example 7

Main entry
> under the title of the document, by **21.7B**

Added entries
> (1) The editor i.e. Doney, by **21.30D**
> (2) The title of the series, by **21.30L**

Unlike the previous item this one is a collection within the terms of rule 21.7, hence main entry is under title. However two points need to be stressed. On the one hand some works qualify as collections rather than as cases of diffuse (i.e.

shared authorship) apparently on the strength of an editor being associated with the work. On the other hand, and as the previous example shows, the appearance of an editor on the title-page certainly does not mean that rule 20.7 is applicable.

Example 8

Main entry
>   under the first named author i.e. Mr K., by **21.25A**, **21.5C** and **21.6C1**

Added entries
(1) The second author i.e. Mrs K., by **21.30B**
(2/3) Under each of the reporters, by **21.29B**
(4) The title of the document, by **21.30J**

The main entry involves a three-stage decision. First it is necessary to determine whether the reporters might qualify as the authors and the algorithm leads to a solution on this point via the 'collaborative new works' route, the decision turning on the information (supplied) that the words are those of the couple interviewed. The status of authors identified only by initials must next be resolved in case the work should rank as anonymous. The section dealing with 'unknown, uncertain, or unstated authorship' is the relevant one here. Finally there is a simple instance of shared authorship.

Example 9

Main entry
>   under the title of the document, by **21.1A2/21.1B2** and **21.6C2**

Added entries
(1) First named author i.e. Donella Meadows, by **21.6C2**
(2) The Club of Rome, by **21.30E**

A two-stage decision is involved. The criteria for corporate authorship are stated in the code and repeated within part 1 of the algorithm. Consulting them will be an important element in dealing with several examples from this point on. In this case main entry under the Club of Rome is eliminated by virtue of the fact that the views expressed are clearly those of the researchers. The next step is to follow the shared authorship route down the left-hand pathway of the appropriate page i.e. more than three authors is resolved by main entry under title, there being no principal author.

Example 10

Main entry
>   under the Institute, by **21.1B2(a)**

Added entries
>   arguably none. It is very unlikely that a report of this nature will be sought

through personal name headings. There is also a case for omitting the title entry by reference to **21.30J(1)**, though the phrase 'essentially the same as the main entry heading' allows some minor differences of interpretation.

Example 11

Main entry
> under the title of the document, by either **21.1C(2)** or **21.7A(3)**. The possibility of corporate authorship should first be considered as Vacation-Work is more than simply the publisher. However there is difficulty in clearly applying any of the criteria of **21.1B2** and, 'in case of doubt' the cataloguer is instructed not to treat as corporate authorship.

Added entries
> (1) The corporate body i.e. Vacation-Work, by **21.30E**
> (2) The editor i.e. Moon, by **21.30D**

Example 12

Main entry
> personal author i.e. Newall, by **21.1A2/21.1B2**

Added entries
> (1) The corporate body i.e. the division of the Ministry, by **21.30E**
> (2) The title of the document by **21.30J**

Various references are required for the corporate body (see section 3). Note that the decision as between a personal author and a corporate body is always a process of elimination in relation to the criteria for main entry under the latter.

Example 13

Main entry
> under the name of the conference, by **21.1B2(d)**

Added entries
> (1) The heading for the Commission, by **21.30E**
> (2) The title of the series, by **21.30L**
> (3) The title of the document, by **21.30J**

In this instance both the contenders for the main entry are corporate bodies. The solution is consistent with the code's general conception of authorship since the opinions expressed at a conference are clearly those of the participants rather than of the convening body i.e. the Commission in this case.

Example 14

Main entry
> under a uniform title for the Buddhist scriptures, by **21.37A**

Added entries
  (1) The translator i.e. Woodward, by **21.30K1**
  (2) The title-page title, by **21.30J**

This example should be identified as a special case i.e. a type of work separated out from the generality of documents because of certain peculiar difficulties which it presents to the cataloguer.

Example 15

Main entry
  under the compiler i.e. Elder, by **21.28B**

Added entries
  (1) The uniform title for the part and version of the Bible to which the concordance relates, by **21.30G**
  (2) The title of the concordance, by **21.30J**

The relevant part of the New English Bible itself occurs in section 2. The student should compare the final solutions for the two items. The algorithm identifies it as a related work and the continuation leads via the elimination of sequels and librettos to a direction requiring other instances of this category to be entered under their own headings i.e. not to be treated as subordinate to the works to which they relate.

Example 16

Main entry
  under the corporate body which the official, in this case the Pope, represents (i.e. the heading for his church); rule **21.4D1**

Added entries
  (1) The publishers, by **21.30E**
  (2) The title of the document, by **21.30J**
  (3) The cover title, by **21.30J**
  (4) The personal heading for this particular pope, by **21.4D1**

Consideration of a series entry for encyclical letters is appropriate. However 21.30L permits a judgement about whether a 'useful collocation' will be achieved and it is felt that an explanatory reference may be sufficient in this case. (See section 3.) The logic of the algorithm is to identify the Pope as a prima facie personal author, but subsequently to single out the fact that he is writing in 'an official capacity' as head of his church as determining main entry under the latter.

SECTION 2

For examples 17-32, using both parts of the algorithm and quoting actual headings in conformity with chapters 22-6 of the code. Main entries are given first in all cases.

Example 17

Headings
> Popper, Karl R
> The logic of scientific discovery

This straightforward example illustrates some basic points about personal name entries which will not subsequently be referred to since they apply to such a large range of headings. **22.5A** directs that entry shall normally be under surname. **22.3A** concerns fullness of name and is important in ensuring standardization of a name for entry purposes. **22.12B** extends the question of fullness to titles of honour. In this instance the author is not entered as 'Popper, Sir Karl R.' because the title is not used in his publications.

The stages of the algorithm for personal name headings is broadly threefold and consists of deciding (a) which of any alternative names for the same person shall be the one selected for entry purposes; (b) the exact form, and order of elements in the preferred name and; (c) prescribed additions to the name. References from unused names or formulations of the name will be required in accordance with chapter 26.

Example 18

Headings
> Baars, F. J. J. Van
> Van Baars, F. J. J.
>> *see* Baars, F. J. J. Van
> Schoot, J.G.J.A. Van der
> Van der Schoot, J.G.J.A.
>> *see* Schoot, J.G.J.A. Van der
> Engels Nederlands woordenboek

A case of shared authorship involving two Dutch names with prefixes. The first author provides main entry by **21.6C1**. **22.5D1** (Dutch) directs entry under the part following the prefix, with reference from the latter by **26.2A3**. Note that the language to which a name belongs is determined by the predominant language of the author and not by its etymology (see also **22.3B**).

Example 19

Headings
> Mao, Tse-tung
>> [Selections]
> Fremantle, Ann

Mao Tse-tung provides a good example of a non-western name. Note that, although detailed provision is made for names in some languages it is also necessary to rely on general rules about entry elements. **22.4B2** is appropriate here and **25.9** is applicable for a uniform title under selections. The added entry under title is obviously redundant in this case, by **21.30J(1)**.

Example 20

Headings
    Leonardo da Vinci
      [Selections]
    Vinci, Leonardo da
      see Leonardo da Vinci
    Taylor, Pamela
    The notebooks of Leonardo da Vinci

The work is preferred under Leonardo rather than da Vinci by **22.8A**, which directs as to form of name when there is no surname in the modern sense. **26.2A3** covers references from parts of a name which might be sought though not chosen as the entry element.

Example 21

Headings
    Fraser, Antonia
    Pakenham, Antonia
      see Fraser, Antonia
    Quiet as a nun

A straightforward example which brings out two points of importance. Firstly, as the author does not use her title in her writings it can be ignored in formulating the heading. Relevant rules are **22.1A**, **22.1B** and **22.12A**. (References would have been required if the title had generated a different entry element). Secondly, since she has written both under her maiden and under her married name, **22.2B** can be consulted for cases involving change of name. The reference is needed by **26.2A1**.

Example 22

Headings
    Spon's mechanical and electrical services price book
    Davis, Belfield & Everest (Firm)

21.1C2 or **21.7A3** seem appropriate in choosing main entry. An added entry is needed under the firm by **21.30E**. The nature of this corporate heading is probably clear enough, but **24.4B** permits the explanatory term as an addition.

Example 23

Headings

> Gibbs-Smith, Charles Harvard
> Smith, Charles Harvard Gibbs-
>   *see* Gibbs-Smith, Charles Harvard
> Great Britain. Science Museum
> Science Museum
>   *see* Great Britain. Science Museum
> A brief history of flying

Personal authorship is preferred as none of the criteria of **21.1B2** apply. **22.5C3** gives a straightforward direction on the form of headings for hyphenated names and **26.2A3** covers the reference. **24.18(3)** is the basis for the form of entry for the Science Museum. In terms of the algorithm the Science Museum is seen as a government agency (but not one of the 'special cases' identified) and as having a name which might be used by a similar agency of another government. A reference from the direct approach to the name is provided for by **26.3A7**.

Example 24

Headings

> Library Advisory Council (England)
> Great Britain. Department of Education and Science. Library Advisory Council (England)
>   *see* Library Advisory Council (England)
> Great Britain. Library Advisory Council (England)
>   *see* Library Advisory Council (England)
> Library Advisory Council (Wales)
>   (with analogous references)
> A report on the supply and training of librarians

Since the basic rule, **24.1**, instructs direct entry for corporate bodies, the cataloguer's main task when faced with a relationship between two or more bodies (in this case between the Councils and the Department) is to check certain other rules which specify exceptions to the norm. Of these **24.12** covers subordinate bodies generally, but gives a reference to **24.18** in the case of government agencies. This rule lists types of corporate body for which direct entry is not appropriate. The Library Advisory Councils are not thought to fall within any of these categories (though type 3 might have been applicable had not the names included the relevant countries), so direct entry is prescribed. **26.3A7** again covers the references.

Example 25

Headings

> Great Britain. Lord Privy Seal

Lord Privy Seal
   see Great Britain. Lord Privy Seal
Privy Seal
   see Great Britain. Lord Privy Seal
Rothschild, Nathaniel Mayer Victor Rothschild, *Baron*
Great Britain. Council for Scientific Policy
Council for Scientific Policy
   see Great Britain. Council for Scientific Policy

The Lord Privy Seal is a government official and an example under this heading is quoted at **24.20E**. **22.6A** determines the form of heading for Rothschild (since he is referred to by his title). Indirect entry for The Council for Scientific Policy is again a judgement based on **24.18(3)** and clearly in doubtful cases this is the safer solution.

Example 26

Headings

Debussy, Claude Achille
L'Orchestre de la Suisse Romande
Ansermet, Ernest
Petite Suite

21.1A1 provides an indication of how the concept of authorship is extended to cover works other than documents. **21.23A** provides specific instructions on sound recordings, with additional remarks on added entries. Debussy is not treated as a prefixed name since it is always written as one word. The approach via the algorithm for this item is — mixed authorship; modification of another work; sound recording; single work.

Example 27

Headings

The Penguin book of English folk songs
Vaughan Williams, Ralph
Williams, Ralph Vaughan
   see Vaughan Williams, Ralph
Lloyd, A.L.
Folk Song Society
English Folk Dance and Song Society
(In addition to the above two entries *see also* or explanatory references are required in both directions to link the two names)

The algorithm identifies this item as a musical work with words, the direction being to consult rule **21.19A** which specifies that the composer (rather than the author of the words) is to be used as the basis for the main entry. However the fact that this is obviously a collection in both respects (it can also be viewed as extracts, but this analysis is only slightly different and leads to the same place) requires re-entry to the algorithm with a solution via **21.7(1 or 2)** under title. Whilst applying the rules to the words or the music produces the same result in this case the priority of the latter would obviously be significant in situations where a work was a collection in one respect but not in the other.

Entry under the corporate body is justified by **21.30E** and also provides an opportunity to illustrate treatment of a change of name.

Example 28

Headings

Bible, N.T. English. New English. 1961
New Testament
   see Bible. N.T.

An example of a complex uniform title involving a part of the Bible, the heading being built up in four stages as follows:

(a) Bible. N.T. (by **25.18A2**)
(b) Bible. N.T. English (by **25.18A10**)
(c) Bible. N.T. English. New English (by **25.18A11**)
(d) Bible. N.T. English. New English. 1961 (by **25.18A13**)

The decision to use uniform title via the rule for sacred scriptures **21.37A**. The reference is required by **26.4A3**.

The formulation of uniform titles represents one of the most difficult parts both of the code and of the algorithm. The Bible is clearly an example of a work appearing under different titles, which meets the initial criteria for establishing a uniform title. The continuation identifies sacred scriptures as a special group of this kind leading on to a general statement about the use of general reference sources to determine the form. Finally there is an indication of the need to consult rules for particular scriptures.

Example 29

Headings

Carroll, Lewis
   [Alice's adventures in wonderland]
Dodgson, Charles Lutwidge
   see Carroll, Lewis
Carroll, Lewis
   [Through the looking-glass]
Alice's adventures in wonderland, through the looking-glass, and other writings

This work illustrates several points. **22.2C2** warrants preference for Carroll over Dodgson as the 'predominant name' (though **22.2C3** would also give an acceptable result to the extent that his writings fall into two clear categories). The second feature is the use of a uniform title by **25.7**, which is necessary to bring the second work into the position where it will be sought within the author heading. Note the variations that apply if more than two works are involved **(25.10)**.

Example 30

Headings

    Newton, *Sir* Isaac
       [Principia mathematica. English]
    Newton, *Sir* Isaac
       Mathematical principles of natural philosophy
          see Newton, *Sir* Isaac. **Principia** mathematica
    Cajori, Florian
    Mathematical principles of natural philosophy

The use of a uniform title in the original language is based on **25.3A**, and **25.5D** warrants the addition of the language of the work in hand where different. **25.2D2** instructs use of name-title references from variant titles, though only the most useful is actually given above. (Another might be from the full title of the Latin original). Cajori warrants an added entry via **21.30H** if not as translator and there is some case for one under Motte. The algorithm for uniform title proceeds by eliminating from consideration the various special categories and takes us to 'single titles created after 1500', the best known title in the original language providing the solution. The section on additions leads to the direction to add the language of the translation.

Example 31

Headings

    Bernal, J.D.
    The scientific and industrial revolutions
    Bernal, J.D.
    Science in history. 2. The scientific and industrial revolutions
      see Bernal, J.D.
         The scientific and industrial revolutions
    The scientific and industrial revolutions

25.6A1 gives instructions for treating individual volumes of a multi-volume work as single items. The corresponding references are dealt with at **26.4A2**. The algorithm identifies as an individual title consisting of a part of a work. However the compilers were left with some doubts as regards the code's precise intentions here in so far as the phrase 'a separately catalogued part of a work' in the rule quoted might be taken to imply a policy decision rather than an outright instruction about multi-part works.

Example 32

Headings

    Griew, Edward

United Kingdom
[The Theft Act, 1968]
The Theft Act, 1968

As the text of the Act only occupies an appendix the work goes under Griew. However an added entry is appropriate by **21.30M** for the Act itself. The appropriate heading is arrived at via **21.31B1** and **25.15A2**. Note that the uniform title is for the name of the Act, not for the name of the book. The title entry is inapplicable in a dictionary catalogue. (cf item 1). The student should have seen the information for this example as an invitation to treat the text of the Act as requiring an analytical entry and two quite independent consultations of the algorithm.

This completes the specimen examples. However Section 3 which follows provides the headings for Examples 1-16

SECTION 3

1   Dodd, K.N.
Pan piper science series
Computers

Comment
The title entry is not appropriate in a dictionary catalogue

2   Stokoe, W.J.
Burton, Maurice
The Observer's book of wild animals

3   Kiaer, Eigil
Hancke, Verner
Garden flowers in colour

4   Scott, T.H.
Stokoe, W.J.
Step, Edward. Wayside and woodland blossoms
Wild flowers of the wayside and woodland

Comment
21.12B instructs that a 'name-title' entry be made under the original author and **21.30G** indicates that this involves adding the title as part of the heading.

5   Pisanello, Antonio
     Pisano, Antonio di Bartolommeo
         see
             Pisanello, Antonio
     Hill, George F.
     Drawings by Pisanello

6   Voltaire
     Arouet, François-Marie
         see
             Voltaire
     Taylor, F.A.
     Blackwell's French texts
     Lettres philosophiques

7   Descartes: a collection of critical essays
     Doney, Willis
     Modern studies in philosphy

8   K., Mr
     Mr K.
         see K, Mr
     K., Mrs
     Mrs K.,
         see K., Mrs
     Ghertler, Monte
     Palea, Alfred
     The Couple

     Comment
     It is assumed that 'K' is likely to be the initial letter of a real name (given
     the nature of the work), hence **22.10** is referred to rather than **22.11**.
     The references are analogous to examples quoted by the code under these
     rules.

9   The limits to growth
     Meadows, Donella H.
     The Club of Rome

10   Tropical Products Institute (London)

11   The directory of summer jobs
     Vacation-Work
     Moon, Sally

12 Newall, R.S.
Great Britain. Ministry of Public Building and Works. Ancient Monuments
and Historic Buildings.
Ancient Monuments and Historic Buildings
see (the above)
Great Britain. Ancient Monuments and Historic Buildings
see (the above)
Great Britain. Department of the Environment. Ancient Monuments and
Historic Buildings
for earlier publications see (the above)
Stonehenge, Wiltshire

13 Regional Coastal Conference (1967 : York)
Great Britain. National Parks Commission
National Parks Commission.
see Great Britain. National Parks Commission
Great Britain. Countryside Commission
for earlier publications see Great Britain. National Parks Commission
Coastal preservation and development
The coasts of Yorkshire and Lincolnshire

Comment
24.7B specifies the formulation of headings for conferences. **24.18** (Type
2) is the basis for indirect entry of National Parks Commission.

14 Tipitaka
Woodward, F.L.
Some sayings of the Buddha

Comment
Buddhist scriptures are specifically covered by **25.18F**. No sub-heading
of Tipitaka is required as the work consists of selections from various
parts of the Canon.

15 Elder, E.
Bible. N.T. English. New English. 1961
New Testament
see
Bible. N.T.
New English Bible : New Testament concordance

Comment
The added entry follows the main entry for item 28 as regards the uniform
title, thus providing adjacent entries for two related works. Note potential
problems in the dictionary catalogue however since the New Testament
is also the subject of the concordance and the subject heading might very
well be similar to the uniform title.

16   Catholic Church. Pope (1963-1978 : Paul VI)
        Populoro progressio
      Catholic Truth Society (London)
      Paul VI, Pope
      On Fostering the development of peoples
      The Great social problem

Comment

24.27B2 covers the form of heading for official documents of the Roman Catholic Church. **22.8** deals with personal headings not involving a surname.